VIA THE ROUNDABOUT

Record of Margaret, the enslaved family matriach.
See Footnote 56 p 39.

VIA THE
ROUNDABOUT

The Scobie Family's Story of Resolve and
Resilience from 1819 through Emancipation,
the Colonial Era, and beyond.

Beverly Scobie

ABOUT THE AUTHOR

Beverly Scobie is a graduate of the University of the West Indies, the Sir Hugh Wooding Law School and Boston University Genealogical Research Certificate Program. For the past thirty-seven years she has been a resident of Brooklyn, New York, where she continues to research and write her family history. *Via The Roundabout* is her first publication.

ISBN: 978-976-8244-49-9

Written by Beverly Scobie
Design and Layout: Paria Publishing Company Limited
Printing: Ingramspark
Printed in the USA

CONTENTS

Descendants of Joseph Arthur, Sr

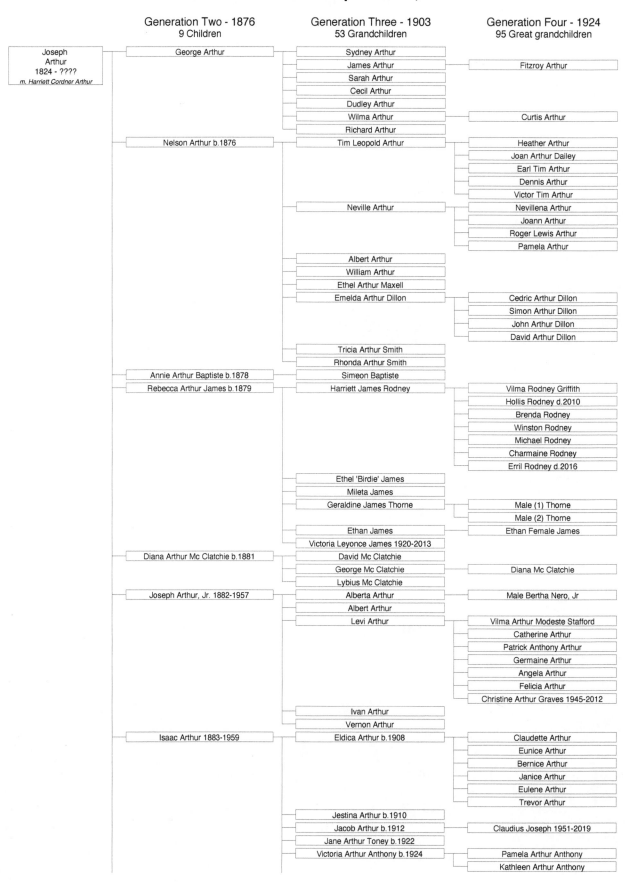

	Generation Two - 1876 9 Children	Generation Three - 1903 53 Grandchildren	Generation Four - 1924 95 Great grandchildren
Joseph Arthur 1824 - ???? *m. Harriett Cordner Arthur*	George Arthur	Sydney Arthur	
		James Arthur	Fitzroy Arthur
		Sarah Arthur	
		Cecil Arthur	
		Dudley Arthur	
		Wilma Arthur	Curtis Arthur
		Richard Arthur	
	Nelson Arthur b.1876	Tim Leopold Arthur	Heather Arthur
			Joan Arthur Dailey
			Earl Tim Arthur
			Dennis Arthur
			Victor Tim Arthur
		Neville Arthur	Nevillena Arthur
			Joann Arthur
			Roger Lewis Arthur
			Pamela Arthur
		Albert Arthur	
		William Arthur	
		Ethel Arthur Maxell	
		Emelda Arthur Dillon	Cedric Arthur Dillon
			Simon Arthur Dillon
			John Arthur Dillon
			David Arthur Dillon
		Tricia Arthur Smith	
		Rhonda Arthur Smith	
	Annie Arthur Baptiste b.1878	Simeon Baptiste	
	Rebecca Arthur James b.1879	Harriett James Rodney	Vilma Rodney Griffith
			Hollis Rodney d.2010
			Brenda Rodney
			Winston Rodney
			Michael Rodney
			Charmaine Rodney
			Erril Rodney d.2016
		Ethel 'Birdie' James	
		Mileta James	
		Geraldine James Thorne	Male (1) Thorne
			Male (2) Thorne
		Ethan James	Ethan Female James
		Victoria Leyonce James 1920-2013	
	Diana Arthur Mc Clatchie b.1881	David Mc Clatchie	
		George Mc Clatchie	Diana Mc Clatchie
		Lybius Mc Clatchie	
	Joseph Arthur, Jr. 1882-1957	Alberta Arthur	Male Bertha Nero, Jr
		Albert Arthur	
		Levi Arthur	Vilma Arthur Modeste Stafford
			Catherine Arthur
			Patrick Anthony Arthur
			Germaine Arthur
			Angela Arthur
			Felicia Arthur
			Christine Arthur Graves 1945-2012
		Ivan Arthur	
		Vernon Arthur	
	Isaac Arthur 1883-1959	Eldica Arthur b.1908	Claudette Arthur
			Eunice Arthur
			Bernice Arthur
			Janice Arthur
			Eulene Arthur
			Trevor Arthur
		Jestina Arthur b.1910	
		Jacob Arthur b.1912	Claudius Joseph 1951-2019
		Jane Arthur Toney b.1922	
		Victoria Arthur Anthony b.1924	Pamela Arthur Anthony
			Kathleen Arthur Anthony

Descendants of Joseph Arthur, Sr (continued)

Generation Two - 1876 9 Children	Generation Three - 1903 53 Grandchildren	Generation Four - 1924 95 Great grandchildren
	Samuel Arthur 1926-2022	Garfield Arthur
		Jonathan Arthur
		Gwenica Arthur
	Delia Rodriguez b.1927	Barbara Rodriguez Regis
	Septimus 'Septie' Arthur 1928-2021	Trevor Arthur Ameron
		Steven Arthur
		Carol Arthur
		Marion Arthur Roberts
		Arlene Arthur
	Greta Arthur b.1930	Jenny Arthur Joseph
		Earl Arthur
		Dawn Arthur
		Chris Arthur
		Chester Arthur
	John Arthur 1932-2021	Lennox Arthur
		Radix Arthur
	Paul Arthur 1934-2017	
	Grace Arthur 1936-1998	Steven Arthur
		Gloria Arthur
Mary Arthur Scobie b.1884	Edward Scobie 1903-1990	Ivy A. Scobie Burrowes d.2005
		Randolph Scobie Richards 1930-2011
		Esmond Scobie 1936-1964
		Eulene Scobie 1938-2012
		Earl Winsor Scobie 1942-2011
	Emelda Scobie Paul 1904-1978	Cassandra Scobie Thompson 1924-2001
	Amelia Scobie Phillip 1908-1996	Karl Phillip
		Molly Phillip Peters 1931-1983
		Knolly Phillip 1933-2013
		Victor Phillip 1935-2004
		Nayleze Reiz Phillip 1937-2020
		Paul Phillip 1939-2014
		Vincent Phillip 1943-2016
	Joseph Scobie 1909-1977	Eunice Scobie
	Alpheus Rudolph Scobie 1910-1986	Carver Milton Scobie
		Winifred Scobie
		Horace Scobie
		Dale Scobie
		Beverly Scobie
		Carlyle Scobie
		Irma Scobie
		Florence Scobie
Cornell Arthur b.1886	Beatrice Arthur Lavington	Eutrice Lavington Johnson
		Ursula Lavington Rennie
		Reginald Lavington
	Leon Arthur	
	James Arthur	
	John Arthur	
	Celestine Arthur Quamina d.1986	Bryan Arthur Quamina
		Brenda Arthur Quamina
	Henry Arthur	Bill Merrit Arthur d.2020
		Victor Arthur
		Eric Arthur
		Ian Arthur
		Earl Arthur
		Millard Arthur 1939-1940
		Dowling Arthur b.1942

Descendants of Margaret Cordner

Generation Two - 1825 3 Children	Generation Three - 1854 3 Grandchildren	Generation Four - 1876 24 Great grandchildren	Generation Five - 1903 85 Descendants

Margaret Cordner b.1797

- Son 1 Cordner b.1825
- Son 2 Cordner b.1826
- Anna 'Ann' Cordner 1833-1901
  - Peter Cordner, Sr. b.1854
    - James Cordner d.1969
    - Angelina E. Cordner Stafford d.1973
      - Una Stafford Quashie d.2015
      - Vida Stafford St. Clair
      - Util Stafford Pavey
      - Amy Stafford Mc Clatchie d.2001
      - Edna Stafford Bruno
      - Herbert Stafford
      - Eula Stafford
      - Rufus Stafford 1926-2010
    - Edward Cordner
    - Peter Cordner, Jr.
    - Ethel Cordner
    - Issac Cordner b.1904
      - Franklyn Cordner d.2014
      - Winston Cordner
      - Jean Cordner d.1998
      - Angela Cordner Tobias d.2017
      - Janet Cordner Scott
      - Joyce E. Cordner Goodridge 1928-2018
      - Ralph Cordner b.1930
      - Roy Cordner 1932-2003
      - Barbara Cordner Williams 1938-2022
    - Lucy Cordner Wheeler 1906-1998
      - Wilma Cordner Wheeler
      - Merle Cordner Wheeler
      - Daphne Cordner Wheeler d.2020
      - Maureen Cordner Wheeler Mattison
      - Victor Cordner Wheeler 1931-2005
      - Olive Cordner Wheeler 1933-2005
      - George Cordner Wheeler 1935-1972
      - Irma Cordner Wheeler b.1937
      - Valentine Cordner Wheeler 1948-2008
    - Ann Cordner 1907-1989
    - Edith Cordner 1913-2007
  - Harriett Cordner Arthur 1855-1930
    - George Arthur
      - Sydney Arthur
      - James Arthur
      - Sarah Arthur
      - Cecil Arthur
      - Dudley Arthur
      - Wilma Arthur
      - Richard Arthur
    - Nelson Arthur b.1876
      - Tim Leopold Arthur
      - Neville Arthur
      - Albert Arthur
      - William Arthur
      - Ethel Arthur Maxell
      - Emelda Arthur Dillon
      - Tricia Arthur Smith
      - Rhonda Arthur Smith
    - Annie Arthur Baptiste b.1878
      - Simeon Baptiste
    - Rebecca Arthur James b.1879
      - Harriett James Rodney
      - Ethel 'Birdie' James
      - Mileta James
      - Geraldine James Thorne
      - Ethan James
      - Victoria Leyonce James 1920-2013
    - Diana Arthur Mc Clatchie b.1881
      - David Mc Clatchie
      - George Mc Clatchie
      - Lybius Mc Clatchie
    - Joseph Arthur, Jr. 1882-1957
      - Alberta Arthur
      - Albert Arthur
      - Levi Arthur
      - Ivan Arthur
      - Vernon Arthur
    - Isaac Arthur 1883-1959
      - Eldica Arthur Winchester b.1908
      - Jestina Arthur Winchester b.1910
      - Jacob Arthur Winchester b.1912
      - Jane Arthur Toney b.1922
      - Victoria Arthur Anthony b.1924
      - Samuel Arthur 1926-2022
      - Delia Rodriguez b.1927
      - Septimus 'Septie' Arthur 1928-2021
      - Greta Arthur b.1930
      - John Arthur 1932-2021
      - Paul Arthur 1934-2017
      - Grace Arthur 1936-1998
    - Mary Arthur Scobie b.1884
      - Edward Scobie 1903-1990
      - Emelda Scobie Paul 1904-1978
      - Amelia Scobie Phillip 1908-1996
      - Joseph Scobie 1909-1977
      - Alpheus Rudolph Scobie 1910-1986
    - Cornell Arthur b.1886
      - Beatrice Arthur Lavington
      - Leon Arthur
      - James Arthur
      - John Arthur
      - Celestine Arthur Quamina d.1986
      - Henry Arthur
  - Rebecca Cordner Saunders b.1857
    - Charlie Saunders
      - Sammy 'Po' Saunders
      - Danny Saunders
    - Daniel Saunders
    - Margaret 'titi' Saunders
      - Jestina Saunders
    - Sally Saunders
    - Simon Saunders d.1964
      - Matilda Saunders d.2002
      - Frederica Saunders d.2021
      - Caroline Saunders Joseph
    - Martha Saunders

In memory of ancestors, my parents Alpheus and Isabella Scobie, my late cousin Samuel Arthur, and acknowledgement of relatives and friends who supported me in this venture.

Old Sangre Grande Police Station with Poui Tree overhanging facade. Appendix 1 (b)

Cunapo, the Nerve Centre of Sangre Grande

The Court House was reconstructed during the first quarter of the 1900s, and converted to a two-story building to accommodate the Warden's Office on the first floor and the Magistrate's Court on the lower floor. 2013 Photo

Foster Road starts mere yards away from the Police Station (the blue wall on the left). Photo shows traffic moving through the Roundabout Hub. 2013 Photo

Façade of Police Station with building housing Warden's Office and Magistrate's Court barely visible on the left. 2013 Photo

Images of Arima and Sangre Grande in the 1960s: Arima Railway Station, Sangre Grande Police Station, Sangre Grande Bus Depot, and a Bus going to Sangre Grande.

(Photos: Paria Archives, Fern Mackenzie Collection)

INTRODUCTION

I am Beverly Scobie, the youngest of eight siblings, four boys and four girls. My parents Alpheus and Isabella Scobie were both from Tobago. I was told that before I was born, my parents and siblings had moved around Trinidad, Tobago and Grenada, as a result of my father's occupation as a colporteur—a purveyor of religious books. In the 1950s our family eventually settled in Sangre Grande where I was born and where I spent my formative years.

Sangre Grande is a small town at the end of the Eastern Main Road, a major artery in the island's transportation system. The artery runs from Port-of-Spain, the capital of Trinidad in the west, to Sangre Grande in the east, a distance of some twenty-eight miles. The very first address that I knew of, No. 1 Foster Road, was an unintentional but highly strategic location, conveniently located a few steps away from the Roundabout,[1] a pulsating hub of activity in the middle of Cunapo, the business district of Sangre Grande. The landmark Roundabout, overlooked by the Police Station[2] marked the convergence of the Toco Main Road and the Eastern Main Road. Mere yards away were other important stops, the Railway Station,[3] and later the Bus Depot,[4] all stops which gave travellers convenient access to our home.

Visitors frequently dropped by our home to see *"Brother Scobie," "Sister Scobie,"* or *"the children."* Depending on their age or relationship, relatives called for Uncle Alpheus, Cousin Alpheus, or Alpheus. In my adult years, I realised that my parents were very hospitable and, I daresay, fairly popular; they entertained in their home in the 1950s and 1960s, which belied perceptions at the time of being devout Christians and aloof people. Many of my contemporaries did not entertain visitors at their homes.

---

1   The Roundabout located in the middle of Cunapo, the business district of Sangre Grande, was an elevated, white, circular island, the middle of a three-pronged hub, around which traffic flowed.... Appendix I (a)

2   Appendix I (b).

3   The Trinidad Government Railway existed between 1876 and 28 December 1968. It was originally built to connect Port-of-Spain with Arima, and was extended to Cunapo (now Sangre Grande) in 1897.

4   The Bus Depot is the terminal point of the Public Transport Service Corporation (PTSC) service in Sangre Grande. The PTSC was established in 1965; it is a state-owned entity providing rapid transport service to the public.

Naturally, my curiosity was piqued from a very early age by these relatives and my parents' friends, many of whom I got to meet as they dropped by our home to visit. Except for my father's siblings and their children, I could not tell how the majority of relatives who visited were related to us. I questioned my mother about our visitors, but even more so about our relatives. Some of the stories she told stirred my interest, but as I grew older, apart from sporadic bursts of enthusiasm to hear more, and occasional jottings to prompt recall, I did not do much more with the information.

My interest in our family's ancestry did not totally disappear, but was sustained for many years thereafter by my mother who had a million stories to tell, some about herself and others about relatives. One day my mother amazed me by mentioning that she knew her great-grandmother who had been enslaved! I was surprised and excited at this revelation and wanted to learn more about her great-grandmother and slavery. I would have to find out on my own because my mother could not recall much more than what she had been told. I also noted that my mother's maiden name was Scobie which was quite an uncommon name. By the time I was old enough to ask how a Scobie had married a Scobie, neither parent could explain in a coherent way how they were related. The rather unusual circumstance of both parents having the same uncommon surname, and not being able to pinpoint the origins of their relatedness, heightened my interest in getting to know who was who.

My fascination with my parents' background led me to delve deeper into my ancestry. One of my goals was to explain to my parents how they were related and to find as much information as I could about the ancestry of my great-great grandmother. It was then I realised that I really did not know very much about my father's parents, especially about his maternal ancestry. Although my father could not fully trace his ancestry, he knew that he and my mother had relatives in common. He had a rather amusing way of assigning the ones he did not care for to my mother. "Your mother's family," he would say with reference to a tiresome cousin.

 It took some time (and research) before I could tell which relatives were held in common and which were not. My father was not one for much conversation about the past. My mother, on the other hand, quite liked telling stories. Not only did she answer my questions to the best of her recollection, she also added bits and pieces of information that she thought might be of interest.

In 2009, I created a family tree.[5] It helped to pinpoint some of my father's maternal ancestors, the Cordners and Arthurs. Margaret, the enslaved family matriarch had a daughter Anna, by her owner Arthur Cordiner. Anna had three children: Peter, Rebecca Saunders née Cordner, and Harriet Arthur née Cordner. Harriet married a formerly enslaved Joseph Arthur, from Barbados, and they had nine offspring: George, Nelson, Annie, Rebecca, Diana, Joseph,

---

5   https://Scobies.tribalpages.com

Isaac, Mary (my father Alpheus Scobie's mother) and Colonel. The marriage of Joseph Arthur and Harriet Cordner linked the Arthur, Cordner and Saunders families, forming a significant part of my father's maternal lineage.

Many of these ancestors were born in Tobago and migrated to Trinidad where they settled in the Toco region.[6] They were part of the labour force that sought work on the Toco estates following the decline in Tobago's once robust economy after Emancipation. Beginning with Peter Cordner in 1887, several families eventually settled in Toco. The last notable of these was Isaac Arthur, my father's uncle, in 1926. My father and his siblings had already arrived there in 1910.

I realised that I had discovered more than the names of my relatives. They were, in fact, pioneers in the development of the Toco region between the 1890s and, more specifically between the 1920s and 1950s when Isaac Arthur made lasting contributions to the establishment of Rampanalgas Village, Toco.[7] I had also found out that Toco was the major port of entry for people coming from Tobago and other Windward islands[8] in the late nineteenth and early twentieth century.

This book is the story of my ancestors and myself. It is pieced together from my personal recollections, those of older relatives and public records. It begins with my own memories of some of the many relatives who visited our home at No. 1 Foster Road. I have given their names and their relationships to my father, and some accounts of their visits. Next, I present some historical figures including my grandmother.

The book is also about my ancestors' contribution to Toco in its transition from a slave plantation community to an agricultural region populated by free men. The Setting focuses on Toco in the early twentieth century. It relies heavily on the accounts of historians, sociologists, writers and the like, whose work I have cross-referenced in giving as brief a summary of the historical context without sacrificing pertinent details; and Isaac Arthur and his family. In the final section I write about my father, Alpheus Scobie and our family at No. 1 Foster Road.

Beverly Scobie

---

6   The Toco Region comprises a string of villages running from west to east along the northern coastline of Trinidad, from Matelot, through Grande Riviere, Sans Souci, and Toco where it peaks at Galera Point. It continues south along the north-eastern coastline from Cumana, Guayamara, Rampanalgas, Balandra and ends in Matura.

7   Toco Village is a distinct area within the Toco Region; located at the confluence of the Caribbean Sea and the Atlantic Ocean. It is the most northeasterly village on the island of Trinidad, and the closest point to Tobago which lies some 22 miles to its north-east.

8   "From 1833 Tobago was administered with Grenada, St. Vincent and Barbados as part of the Windward Islands, whose seat of government was in Barbados; St. Lucia was added to the Windward Islands administration in 1838."
Craig-James, Susan, E. The Changing Society of Tobago, 1838-1898 A Fractured Whole. Volume I: 1838-1900 p 61.

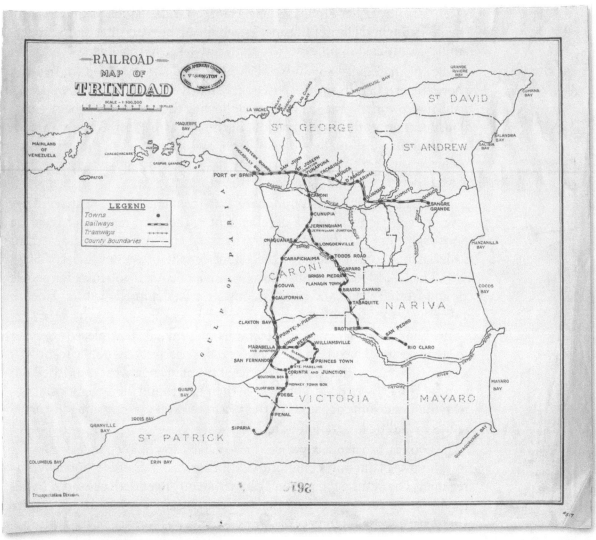

Above:

The railway line to Arima opened up the east west corridor, making it easier to transport estate produce from the north-east to Port-of-Spain markets.

THE WRITER

I was born on a Saturday morning at Nexter Trace, Sangre Grande, Trinidad. My mother did not make it to church that morning. I was told that the *tapia* house[9] where I was born was destroyed by a devastating earthquake which struck the island sometime after my birth.

My parents were forced to find other accommodation for their large family. It seems that because of the size of our family, we were given preferential treatment, and were allowed to live at the unoccupied train master's residence, a house on Brierley Street, Sangre Grande, near to the Railway Station.

This accommodation was temporary, and after a few hiccups, our family finally settled at No. 1 Foster Road, one street away from the Cunapo Roundabout. On one occasion, I visited the area where I was born, I was unable to locate either the street or trace which both seemed to have disappeared into nothingness. When I visited my old home at No.1 Foster Road, the street sign was in place, but the house at No. 1 had been replaced.

I cannot say for certain when I became fascinated by the past. Perhaps it was when I was a small child and my mother told me stories about her childhood; or maybe it was when I became aware that my parents had the same surname and I wanted to know how this came to be. I know that I was intrigued by the relatives who visited us and wondered about their lives. When I was a high school student[10] I studied West Indian History and learned about slavery; the slave trade; the horrors of the Middle Passage, and life on the Caribbean plantations. I knew for certain that some of my ancestors had undergone these terrible experiences.

My first serious attempt to document what I knew of my family's genealogy came when I was a Registrar of Births and Deaths at the Red House,[11]

---

9 The *'tapia'* house, made of earth, grass and other organic material was restyled as dictated by the times and circumstances. Various iterations of the structure emerged, for example, the tapia was camouflaged with other materials to conceal the mud walls; galvanised roofing was added, and later electrical wiring was added for lighting. See photos on pages 80-81. and Appendix III (a)

10 High School Student Appendix IX (d)

11 Trinidad's historic Red House is situated in the heart of downtown Port-of-Spain. It was painted a distinct red colour, said to date back to the 1897 Jubilee for Queen Victoria. The original building was burnt to the ground during the 1903 Water Riots, and replaced in 1907 by a building which retained the colour and name. The building was the seat of Parliament, and also housed the offices of the Attorney-General, Registrar-General where I worked, Lands & Surveys Department, Judges' Chambers, the Courts of Justice and Law Libraries.

Port-of-Spain. This position gave me access and was my introduction to public records. During my eighteen months there, between 1980 and 1982, I made the effort to compile dates and names. It became apparent to me that without a clear idea of whom to look for and the dates to look at, the task of locating ancestors was almost impossible. I retrieved a few names, but not quite as many as I would have liked. Even with my mother's input I did not get very far.

In 2009 when I created a family tree, it helped me to better place relatives, some of whose stories were so fascinating that I decided to further research the more intriguing characters and the times in which they lived. This was when I took a second look at the family tree, and did a serious assessment of who and what was needed. The display of information in this format was revealing as it highlighted missing relatives; some who showed up in unexpected places; others thought to be related but were not; and still others left dangling from one single parent, as I struggled to locate the next. Recurring gaps of nameless persons prompted me to seek out relatives, particularly older ones who might fill in some of the gaps, while I captured their recollections before they were lost. Little did I know that this undertaking would involve so much more than adding stories to names. It took years of on and off research before I could even put together a reasonable semblance of my findings. Because my father's relatives were in rapid decline, I decided to start by documenting what I found of his maternal ancestry.

Few of my father's older relatives were alive, and it took years of persistence to find those who were willing to share information, or be persuaded to share what they wished to share. I now had the task of connecting and arranging the fragments of what I was told into a coherent family history.

This journey led to my reconnection in December 2009, with Victoria Leyonce James *'Cousin Lee,'*[12] whom I first met in 1971. Cousin Lee's mother Rebecca James née Arthur (Aunt Becca), and Mary Scobie née Arthur, my father's mother, were sisters. I mentioned my interest in meeting some of our other older relatives to gather information about my father's mother and her side of the family. Cousin Lee shared information which whetted my appetite for more, and caused me to question what I had been told of Mary, my father's mother. Cousin Lee mentioned, "You should talk to your cousins, the Arthur men." She said this with a mischievous smile.

Between 2010 and 2014, I connected with a number of relatives,[13] some of whom I met for the first time, some I had heard of, and others I already knew. In 2011, I located Samuel Arthur[14], the son of Isaac Arthur, one of Mary and Rebecca's brothers. By the time I met him in person while on a visit to Trinidad in 2017, Samuel and I were familiar with each other, having exchanged family

---

12   Appendix VI (b)

13   Appendix VI (b)

14   Appendix II (a)

stories during our many telephone conversations. I described efforts I had made to document our family history, and he agreed to do DNA testing to assist in establishing the origins of our common lineage, a way of showing relatedness and correctly identifying our origins.

While it sometimes happens that important details get lost in the telling and retelling of stories, I thought it better to preserve what I found. Cordner children and their descendants passed on stories of Margaret, the family matriarch. Margaret's story retained sufficient information for me to identify, connect, and place persons and events mentioned within their historical context. This helped me to authenticate accounts which might otherwise seem outlandish with documentary evidence that confirms the existence of these ancestors and their times. I chanced upon Joseph Arthur, another ancestor whom I had not heard of. The relatives to whom I spoke were oblivious to his existence because no one had mentioned him. This was an unexpected find for me, as I established his place among my ancestors.

Descendants who left Tobago to work on the cocoa estates of Sans Souci, Toco, brought the ethos of ancestors, asserting themselves as proud, vibrant people who helped to shape what for them was a new environment. They did what they knew best, toiling away to carve out portions of land where they and their families could thrive. Demographic evidence of their existence is captured in the Island's Births, Deaths, Marriages, and Land Deed Registers, which may appear sterile to future generations as they do to me now. Here I am supplementing those demographics by telling some of their stories.

Why is it important for me to relate my family's history? Margaret and Joseph Arthur were sons and daughters who once enslaved were looked upon as *Chattel*—a piece of property to be bought, sold, given, inherited. They had no voice. Mostly viewed as an amorphous collective, their humanity, essence and individuality were smothered by the brutal practices of chattel slavery, the traumatic effects of which is evident in descendant generations. They reflect the larger diaspora of souls whose names may not be known, and whose stories may never be told, but who similarly endured the Middle Passage and enslavement.

Records of my original ancestors when they exist, are in Slave Registers![15] Records used to assess compensation due to owners deprived of their means of livelihood; now the only source of documented information concerning ancestors, some of whose names I had barely heard. Stark brittle, crumbling pages in cold archives which quantify their existence but nullify their humanity. My ancestors were enslaved people who, for the most part, are reduced to one line generic abbreviations. By writing their stories I hope to restore the essence of their spirit and humanity; to amplify their presence

---

15   Office of Registry of Colonial Slaves and Slave Compensation Commission: Records; (The National Archives Microfilm Publication T71); Records created and inherited by HM Treasury; The National Archives of the UK (TNA), Kew, Surrey, England; Slave Registers of former British Colonial Dependencies from 1813–1834.

with a sense of gravity, if only for the time spent reading about them, allowing future generations a backward glance to connect to legendary ancestors.

I am mindful that the main characters are identifiable and connected to relatives who are alive. With that in mind, I have avoided calling the names of living persons whenever possible in the body of the text, mostly referencing them as footnotes.

Beverly Scobie,
Sangre Grande - 1956

Beverly standing against the mesh wire fence - 1961

VISITING RELATIVES

It was the early 1960s and I was almost seven years old. The mesh wire fence which enclosed our yard curved outwards, as I leaned against it, peering at the date palms that fell outside of the fencing, just beyond my grasp. I would run to open the gate when I caught sight of any of our relatives or friends coming towards the house. Sometimes they would see me before I saw them, in which case they would call out to me. I was always happy to see relatives, especially Daddy's.

They travelled what seemed considerable distances to see us, about twenty-five miles from Cumana Village where most of them still lived, along the Toco Main Road to Sangre Grande. The mode of transportation at the time was either a PH (private hired) taxi carrying four or five adult passengers, (or more if children were a part of the trip), and the infrequent government bus.

The journey along the Toco Main Road seemed longer than the forty-five-minute drive through winding roads that did not see much upkeep. Along the way hills popped up and just as suddenly plunged into rocky inclines, threatening motion sickness. The verdant forests which flanked the route were sometimes truncated, replaced with meagre guard rails running along unsheltered portions of the path. In places the sheer drop to the barrier of dark jagged rocks below was clearly visible at low tide. Those on the passenger side of the transport turned away from the vertigo-inducing spell to stare inland at occasional clusters of tiny houses, or just a single one, precariously perched against the hills: a reminder to travellers that civilisation existed here too. I found this out on my first trip to vacation camp when I was older.

The bus depot was a less than ten minute walk to our home. Whichever mode of transport was used, it was easy to manoeuvre one's way through the bustle of Cunapo to get to the sanctuary of our home.

Daddy's relatives invariably brought us treats. Male relatives seemed to prefer giving us loose change: two bobs, or twenty-five cent pieces. At the time a *bob* would buy a tub of Cannings Ice Cream, or an eleven cents bottle of Red or Orange Solo, (we weren't allowed to drink Pepsi or Coke), a coconut drop for one penny, leaving enough change to buy candy—Trebor,

5

Butter-nut, Five-For-Cent, Sour-Sweet, and Diana Mints with little love notes on the wrapping paper, and yes, we tithed; ten percent of whatever money we got went to church offerings.

Female relatives brought us home-made goodies. *sugar-cake*, made of grated or chipped coconut cooked in sugar, spices and cloves; *tollum*, where the grated coconut was cooked in molasses; *bene balls*, a delicious candy made of sesame seeds; *chilibibi* made of yellow corn grains parched then ground with brown sugar into a fine, delicious, chewy powder. Our aunts made funnel-shaped packages with brown shop paper, which they filled with heaps of *chilibibi*. We ate the sweet powder by pinch, lick and scoop, while trying to avoid it entering the nostrils. They also brought us seasonal fruits like *pommecythere*, *sugar apple*, *governor* and *chili plums*, *mangoes*, and *mandarins*, anything they could put their hands on, *"for the little-ones."* I was the number one little one, being the last child in the family.

Auntie *"Melia"* Amelia, Daddy's older sister, seemed to always carry a strong smell of green limes about her. The green lime smell was inadvertently solved many years later, when her granddaughter mentioned one of the things her grandma did to make do, "Mama said, 'Before we had deodorant we rubbed green limes on the underarms.'"[16] Auntie Melia would pull a chair and sit as soon as she entered the house, while taking off her hat and fanning herself. After a few minutes of catching her breath, she would put her purse to one side and rummage through her market bag to find the goodies she brought us. I hovered nearby with bated breath, eager to see the contents of her bag.

Joseph Scobie, *"Uncle Joe"* Daddy's older brother, a carpenter by trade, was said to be the son who most closely resembled their father. His shy demeanour caused the less observant to miss the reflexive action of his left hand which retreated to his side when not in use. It was a learned action to conceal the knobs of the thumb, index and middle fingers of that hand, remnants of the dynamite explosion which had disfigured his limb when he was twelve years old. It was said that he found a stick of explosives which looked to him like a pencil case, among his father's tools. Unable to prise it open with bare fingers, he attempted to open it by pounding the explosive with a stone.

Aunt Annie, Daddy's Aunt, was a tall, maybe 5'10", red-skinned, slender lady with thick, long, white plaits. She may have been a little erratic, which was my childish perception. Not that I recall seeing her doing anything erratic.

Cousin *"Sim"* Simeon, her son, was a big hunk of a teddy bear who played the piano so well despite the width of his fingers, each about the thickness of a sausage. In addition, he had a huge supernumerary on each hand, making twelve fingers in all. These additional fingers jiggled with such confidence

---

16   Baking soda was rubbed under the arms as deodorant and ground charcoal was used as toothpaste, both of which were later commercialised for the same use.

as he played the piano, eliciting just as much attention, if not more, than the chords he struck. It was fascinating to watch, I could not peel my eyes away from these mesmerising digits as I wandered around the piano seat to observe if the other supernumerary executed a similar jiggle.

Cousin Sydney, another of Daddy's cousins, was just about as big as Cousin Simeon, and somewhat darker brown in complexion. Maybe it was just his journeyman's clothing or as my mother would say, "the terrible midday heat," that accounted for his rumpled appearance. He was even more jovial and friendly than Simeon, leading me to suspect that he was just downright noisy from the way his voice would suddenly drop, or unexpectedly grow louder, as he tried to "keep it down" when visiting Cousin Alpheus. He did not come by often, and when he did it was, "Cousin Alpheus, I'm just stopping by to say howdy, but I have to leave now," probably taking a chance in between catching buses, to drop by to see "cousin Alpheus and the children."

Cousin Bertha, Daddy's cousin, was the daughter of his mother's brother, Joseph Arthur. She was as tall as Aunt Annie, with a similar slender build, and light brown in complexion. The permanent furrowing of her brows, even when not frowning, gave her face a quirky, impish expression which made one unsure of her mood. I seem to think that she cussed a lot even though I had never heard her; she would not dare to cuss in my Daddy's house. On second thought, I realised much later that my memories of her colourful language were influenced by an incident she reported to mother one day when I was within earshot. "That damn Brizan, quack dentist, just took out my good tooth, not the bad one!" She sounded hopping mad, maybe the cocaine[17] used for the extraction had worn off, as I deciphered her muffled ranting through a bloody mouth stuffed with gauze and cotton. Mother did not respond but I could see the way she *cushoo*[18] her mouth. I suspect she may have wanted to smile, but chose to stay silent.

Auntie *"Becca"* Rebecca, was Auntie Annie's sister, another of Daddy's aunts. She was not as tall or as light as her sisters, but played up her attractiveness by always dressing tastefully. I recall her wearing print pleated dresses, featuring belts of the same fabric, and little hats that barely covered the crown of her head. These were some of the relatives who visited us.

Additionally there were other relatives from Cumana who boarded at our home to attend school in Sangre Grande. Our first boarders were Paul Phillip,[19] one of Auntie Amelia's sons, who was jovial and entertaining. His repeated references to *Sir John Barbirolli*,[20] whose name he constantly dropped, while avidly pursuing violin lessons, caused us to refer to him as

---

17   Cocaine, an anaesthetic, was commonly used in dentistry to produce numbness before surgery.

18   Any furtive gesture with the mouth intended to mock another person.

19   Appendix VI (b) Paul Phillip

20   Sir John Barbirolli (2 December 1899–29 July 1970) was a British conductor and cellist; He began to play the violin when he was four, and later served as music director of the New York Philharmonic, from 1936 to 1943.

"*Barbirolli*"; and there was Eunice Scobie,[21] Uncle Joe's only child, a quiet soul who plaited my hair in cornrows.

There were day boarders, relatives who did not stay overnight, but travelled to and from Sangre Grande to attend school. They brought their own lunches which they left at our home on the way to school, returning at lunchtime to eat. Linroy Scobie[22] and his sister Gwyneth, with their multi-tiered carriers[23] of food, were day boarders.

It was natural for me to develop an interest in relatives who visited our home as I grew up. Later, I became aware that there were some I had not heard of, and who never came to our home. I suppose that some of the relatives we did not meet may have been separated by religious bias, along with my father's reputation as being strict and stern; he definitely was not about to serve alcoholic beverages or animal flesh at our home. We were always good for a gluten sandwich,[24] and a glass of cold lime juice, as our lime tree, a perennial bearer of fruit, always seemed to be laden with limes.

Even though my father left Cumana Village, he never gave up on his relatives, ensuring that his children knew them as much as possible and that they knew us. We sometimes visited some of them. I recall during August holidays, my older sister and I would take the bus to Port-of-Spain where we caught another bus to San Fernando. Here we spent time with Daddy's brother, Uncle Edward who lived at 3E, Fonrose Street with his family.

Left:
A Government Bus awaits passengers at a bus depot.
(Paria Archives)

---

21   Appendix VI (b) Eunice Scobie Tuitt

22   Appendix VI (b) Linroy Scobie

23   Tiffin carriers, a type of stacked lunch box usually three tiers, made from aluminium or enamel, used to carryfood.

24   A vegetarian food made from the protein gluten, the residual product after the starch was washed from dough. The gluten was seasoned and boiled with marmite, which gave it a meat-like consistency.

Uncle Edward with his wife Ella and daughter Eulene.

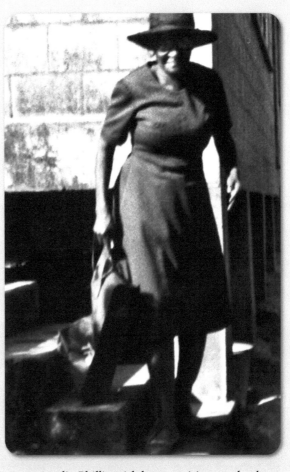

Aunt Amelia Phillip with her promising market bag.

*Uncle
Joseph Scobie*

*1965 Paul "Pablo" "Barbirolli" Phillip,
Amelia's son.*

Above:
Home made Tollum by author. Grated coconut cooked in molasses.

Below:
Sugar apple native to tropical climate in the West Indies.

Above:
Bene balls, a delicious candy made of sesame seeds.

Above:
Sugar-cake, made of grated or chipped coconut cooked in sugar, spices and cloves.

THE SETTING

Tobago, the island from which my father's maternal ancestors migrated during the late nineteenth and early part of the twentieth century, has its own unique and checkered history. Amerindians who first lived on the island, were superseded by European powers: the Duchy of Courland, Dutch, Spanish, French, and English competitors, each laid claim to Tobago.

The Island gained the dubious distinction of having changed hands over thirty times, the most of any of the Caribbean islands. These claims do not take into account the pirates and buccaneers who made the island their base while menacing the Caribbean seas.

Tobago was fully colonised after 1763 when the Treaty of Paris ended the island's status as a neutral territory, temporarily putting an end to French claims and ceding it to British control. British settlers with their African slaves transformed the island into a flourishing plantation economy, entirely dependent on slavery, which lasted until the early nineteenth century. Sugar, rum, cocoa, coffee, indigo and nutmeg were counted among its produce which made the tiny island a prized British possession.

French efforts to gain control of Tobago had temporary success between 1781 and 1793 when they invaded the island and destroyed its sugar plantations. A period of back and forth ensued between the two rivals, with each claiming ownership of the island until Britain regained possession in 1803. The question of ownership was finally settled by the 1814 Treaty of Paris which effectively extinguished all French claims, and Tobago remained a British colony until independence in 1962.

Meanwhile the British slave trade, abolished in name only in 1807, continued to support the importation of slaves into Tobago. Britain revitalised the Tobago plantations after 1814, which resulted in another successful phase of sugar production on the island. The success lasted until 1834 when slavery was abolished and full Emancipation granted to enslaved people in 1838.

The end of slavery and emancipation, precipitated Tobago's rapid economic decline which was worsened by competition from foreign sugar, especially that grown in countries where slaves could still be imported. The collapse of plantation underwriters and a devastating hurricane in 1847 were the final death blows to an already shrinking economy. Those who could, seized the opportunity to travel to the north-eastern region of Trinidad where work was said to be plentiful on the cocoa estates of Sans Souci.

Amerindian - First People

The north-eastern region of Trinidad where relatives migrated was one of the scattered pockets where Amerindians clustered to resist Spanish colonisation following the arrival of Christopher Columbus in 1498. The region was remote, inaccessible, and isolated from the rest of Trinidad. When direct attempts to colonise the native population failed, Spain sent Capuchin priests to establish encomiendas or mission estates in and around the areas they inhabited, ostensibly to Christianise them while forcing them to work on the estates.

Mission estates were established in the Toco Region where large numbers of Amerindians could be found. One mission was established in Toco in 1760, and another a little further to the south of the peninsula at Cumana. These two missions were linked by a track known today as Anglais Road.[25] Two other missions were established in Salybia and Matura.

Spain was unable to effectively harness Amerindian labour to develop the island, notwithstanding the introduction of mission estates. Following years of resistance to Spanish intrusion, the majority of the Amerindian population was now decimated due to war and disease. Spain lacked the funds needed to purchase slaves to develop the island, so that Trinidad remained undeveloped and sparsely populated.[26] There were no large plantations producing crops to sell to Europe.

The 1783 Cedula of Population

positively impacted population growth in Trinidad.

The Spanish King issued the *1777 Cedula of Population* which opened up the island to planters who were Catholic. Most of the planters who responded came from the French Caribbean Islands of Martinique, Guadeloupe, and the formerly French Island of Dominica. Planters also came from Grenada, which even though British, had a large number of French settlers who were Catholic. *The 1777 Cedula* did not attract as many immigrants as Spain had hoped.

To encourage more planters to migrate, the King issued the *1783 Cedula of Population* which was much more attractive to planters. It was crafted by

---

25   Anthony, M. (1988). Towns and Villages of Trinidad and Tobago. Circle Press.

26   In 1782, there were 126 Whites; 295 Coloureds; 310 Slaves and 2,082 Indians. A total population of 2,813. Population statistics Trinidad 1782 – 1810 Gerard A. Besson (2007-12-20). "The Caribbean History Archives - The Royal Cedula of 1783". Paria Publishing Co. Ltd. Retrieved 2022-01-14.

Roume de St. Laurent, a Catholic nobleman who lived in Grenada. He became very influential in the Spanish government of Trinidad, and put forward proposals to develop the island, which the King accepted. *The 1783 Cedula* extended previous incentives, not only to Roman Catholics, but also to subjects of nations allied to Spain. Settlers who swore loyalty to the Spanish Crown were to receive land allotments in sizes depending on their race and heritage, along with generous tax benefits. As a result, French, Irish, German, Italian and English families came to Trinidad. There were Venezuelan[27] families who also came.

Some of the planters were white, others of mixed race (African and European), called *'free coloureds'* They all brought slaves with them. Other Africans were brought directly from Africa on slaving ships.[28]

The French played a critical role in populating[29] the island of Trinidad, and by extension the Toco Region. French immigrants established communities throughout the island, in Blanchisseuse, Champs Fleurs, Paramin, Cascade, Carenage and Laventille. Some settled in the north-east of the island, where, according to Anthony, "The Spanish Governor, Don José María Chacon, establishing clear cut boundaries to seal off the mission from the north-east and eastern areas, granted six parcels of land which we know as Toco today."[30]

In 1797, fourteen years after the *1783 Cedula of Population* took effect, the British captured Trinidad from Spain, which led to another influx of settlers: English, Scots, Irish, German and Italian families.

According to Anthony, when the British entered Toco in 1797, the population consisted of twenty-eight French settlers with a workforce of one hundred and fifty-eight slaves and sixty-two free blacks. One hundred and fifty-five Amerindians were listed as living on the mission which was intact, but this number did not account for those living outside of the mission. An inventory of the same year showed that there was just one sugar mill in the district, while there were as many as fifty-nine cotton mills. The French settlers focused on cotton production, which was the major crop, and the rest of the population turned the village into 'a depot of produce.' There were no roads leading out of the region, which made it extremely difficult to get produce out of the area.[31]

The Abolition of Slavery and Emancipation caused major contractions in the available labour supply on the Island. Other sources of labour were

---

27 Morton-Gittens, Dane. "The Golden Age and Decline of Matelot (1885–1945)" History in Action, Vol. 2 No. 2, September 2011 ISSN: 2221-7886. Dept. of History, The University of the West Indies, St. Augustine, Trinidad and Tobago.

28 Brereton, B. (1996). An Introduction to the History of Trinidad and Tobago. Heinemann Educational Publishers

29 In 1789 there were 2151 Whites; 4,467 Coloureds; 10,100 Slaves and 2,220 Indians. A total population of 18,918. Population statistics Trinidad 1782 – 1810 Gerard A. Besson (2007-12-20). "The Caribbean History Archives - The Royal Cedula of 1783". Paria Publishing Co. Ltd. Retrieved 2022-01-14.

30 Anthony, 1988, p.317.

31 See Anthony, 1988, p. 317.

needed to supplement the number of enslaved people brought to the island during the *Cedula* which had decreased over time by attrition. In the Toco region, the need for labourers was acute, where the remoteness of the region precluded other parts of the island as a source of labour.

Tobagonians were eager to find work, more so after Emancipation in 1838, when the Island's rapid economic decline meant fewer opportunities for work on the island. 'Day Labourers' began travelling from Tobago to Toco by small boats. The trickle of labourers coming to the region gradually increased to a steady stream, as the need for workers multiplied. Apart from Tobagonians seeking work, labourers came from neighbouring islands, Grenada, Barbados, St. Lucia and St. Vincent, when cocoa became profitable. They too hoped to find jobs in the area.

In 1866, Peter Cordner, then a twelve year old boy, first began travelling from Tobago to seek work on the cocoa estates of Sans Souci, Toco. He and fellow labourers continued to risk their lives travelling by small boats on the high seas, the only means of getting to the cocoa estates.

When Peter Cordner first arrived, the region was still predominantly virgin forest, sparsely populated and isolated from the rest of Trinidad. The outlines of tiny enclaves were barely visible in areas where the forests had been cleared. There were no lights, so that after nightfall it became pitch black and silent, except for the occasional flame of a lighted flambeau. There were no roads and labourers walked for miles, most of the time barefooted, through densely wooded forests, on dirt paths created by the footfall of First Peoples. Draft animals, donkeys and mules, were used by those who owned or could afford to pay for this mode of transport.

Despite depleted numbers, the Amerindian influence was evident throughout various aspects of village life. The homes of villagers were made of mud and grass—tapia huts; domestic utensils like the oven used for cooking[32] was made of clay, as were the earthenware vessels used for storing water. Water for domestic use was collected when rain fell or from nearby rivers. Domestic amenities were minimal, like the pallets made from the fibre of husked coconuts and used as mattresses for sleeping. Labourers, when they became more familiar with the Region, erected lean to shacks for overnight accommodation.

Owners of large estates, who lived in other parts of the island like Port-of-Spain, kept estate houses in *"the country"* where they spent time, especially during the harvesting of crops. These estate houses ranged in size from the large wooden structures built bungalow-styled, and comfortably furnished to accommodate the owner, family members and any visiting guests, to smaller more utilitarian houses.

---

32   Appendix III (b) Clay Oven

Apart from the estate house, there was the curious, quaint cocoa house,[33] a structure similar in appearance to a house, built with a mobile roof and a wooden floor to facilitate the processing of cocoa beans. Sometimes the cocoa house was rented out to persons with small plots of land who participated in cocoa cultivation and sold their beans to big owners. The cocoa house also alternated as a copra house for drying coconut kernels. Cocoa houses can still be found today, on former cocoa estates where they are mostly shrouded by tall grasses and shrubs, abandoned.

Labourers from Tobago, some of whom were experienced in growing cocoa at home, augmented, replaced and even outnumbered former slaves. They supplied the workforce necessary to plant, develop and sustain cocoa estates in the region, especially on larger estates. It took some six to eight years to form the core of what would become a cocoa estate. In addition to looking after the cocoa estates, labourers like Peter planted ground provisions such as plantains, sweet potato, cassava, *eddoes* and *dasheen* between the cocoa trees to protect the young saplings from direct sunlight. These provision grounds were a source of food for them, as well as for the Port-of-Spain market where the bulk of the produce was sold.

There was always work, and labourers were kept busy planting, rotating crops, tending cocoa trees, and eventually harvesting, sweating[34] and drying the beans. They and their children looked forward to *dancing cocoa*[35] during harvest time, when they sang *Patois*[36] songs as they *danced* the beans, polishing them in the process. Polished beans were more attractive and fetched higher prices. Some villagers became so adept at *dancing cocoa* that they were able to make extra money by hiring themselves out to dance on other estates.

Tobagonians and Toco

It was all one and the same people.

It is not clear when Toco and Tobago were linked to the *"Round The Island Steamer Service"*[37] which the British introduced to Trinidad in 1818, linking Port-of-Spain to San Fernando. Both Toco and Tobago were subsequently added as regular ports of call, which greatly benefitted the Toco Region. The steamer service facilitated access to Port-of-Spain markets where the bulk of produce coming out of Toco was sold, and it provided a safe form of transportation for short-term labourers from Tobago willing to travel to Trinidad to work the land while maintaining their home base in Tobago.

---

33   Appendix VIII (a) Cocoa House

34   Appendix VIII (b) Sweating Cocoa

35   Appendix VIII (c) Dancing cocoa

36   A mixture of French and African dialect.

37   The 'Round the Island Steamer Service,' was introduced to Trinidad by English Governor Sir Ralph Woodford in 1818. The Steamer Service linked Port-of-Spain to San Fernando. Later other ports of-call were added, which included Tobago and Toco. At the time the Steamer Service was added to Toco, this was the only means of transport in and out of the area.

Tobagonians flooded the Region, so that a depot was set up in Toco Village to accommodate landings, and a police station was built just above the depot to oversee that landings went well.[38]

In 1849, the Region was designated a Ward by the Governor, Lord Harris; the Ward of St. David, with administrative offices located at the Warden's Office in Sangre Grande—the Ward of St. Andrew.

The steady stream of people moving back and forth between the islands fostered the development of a symbiotic relationship between Tobago and Toco where some settled permanently.[39] The Toco Region appeared to be more an extension of Tobago than a part of the island of Trinidad.

It was said that migration from Tobago appeared to have peaked in the 1880s, by which time "all the original settlers and ex-slaves had passed away... Toco was now populated almost entirely by people from Tobago."[40]

Interestingly, Craig-James points out, "There are no records for Tobagonians in Trinidad before 1891."

Tobagonians living in Trinidad between 1891 and 1901 was five times the increase in the Tobago population.[41]

The *people from Tobago,* included Peter Cordner, who migrated during this period, and settled permanently in Redhead, Cumana Village in 1887. Peter's married sisters, Harriet Arthur and Rebecca Saunders, later joined him with their families. Small enclaves of Tobagonians now existed within themselves, except for contact with Tobago and the markets in Port-of-Spain. The enclaves slowly evolved into hamlets, small settlements populated by migrant labourers who developed their own identity, accent, dialect and mannerisms. It was a separate world, a perfect place for those with secrets to hide.

It was customary for a young woman who became pregnant out of wedlock—had a fall, as they said—to be sent to Toco until the child was born. Thereafter she would return to Tobago as though she had simply been visiting relatives in Trinidad. Sometime later, her child who was assumed to be a late born child, would join the family in Tobago. The result was that there are persons who grew up calling their mother, sister, without ever learning the truth. It was not only the Tobagonian lady who found a haven in Toco. I was told of a young lady from Woodbrook, Port-of-Spain, who fell as a young girl and was sent to Toco. When her mother's contemporaries and close relatives identified as being born in Port of Spain, her mother received quizzical looks when she felt pressured to reveal her birthplace as Toco.

It was not only the Tobagonian lady who found a haven in Toco. Some men took the opportunity to maintain two households, one in Tobago and

38   Anthony, 1988, p. 319.
39   Appendix IV
40   Anthony, 1988, p.318.
41   Craig-James, Susan E. The Changing Society of Tobago, 1838-1938 A Fractured Whole, Volume II: 1900-1938 p 189. Appendix IV.

the other in Toco, which solved the puzzle for another friend who often wondered at her uncle who always lived at Tobago having two sons in Toco during the late 1930s, although he had never lived there.

Declining sugar prices led to Tobago's consolidation with other British colonies in the region, the Windward Islands, a loose association which failed to bolster Tobago's shrinking economy. In 1889 Tobago was attached to Trinidad as a ward forming the colony of Trinidad and Tobago, which brought about the end of internal self-government to the island.

"Cocoa Is King"

French Creoles pivoted from cotton production to cocoa, coffee and other crops, taking full advantage of opportunities presented by the British who opened up Crown Lands to persons willing to develop the land. Peter Cordner and other family members took advantage of this opportunity and some family members were recipients of crown grants.[42] After years of toil on the cocoa estates, the family was no longer satisfied to just cultivate the lands with which they had grown familiar, so they purchased them. Cordners, Arthurs, Saunders purchased several acres of coconut estates along the Cumana coastline, and cocoa lands in Anglais and Morne Cabrite, despite competition from wealthy English and other European competitors.

Between the late 1890s and early 1920s cocoa became the number one export from the Toco Region. The total production of cocoa for the island even surpassed that of sugar, Trinidad's most valuable export. A popular saying at the time, *"Cocoa is King,"* captured the enormity of this achievement. "The demand for the high quality beans[43] grown in Trinidad would remain high. Exports had averaged around eight million lbs. a year in 1871–80, by the decade 1911–20 they averaged fifty-six million lbs per annum, a seven fold increase …"[44]

According to Brereton, in *The Book of Trinidad*, the rapid expansion of cocoa as a crop for export can be dated to around 1870 when demand for cocoa in Europe and North America expanded tremendously. Chocolate bars and cocoa as a beverage were consumed on a large scale, the most important reason for its expansion in Trinidad. The opening up of Crown Lands facilitated its expansion.

Estate owners made fortunes, and individual growers were afforded a comfortable lifestyle. Substantial prosperity resulted from the cocoa boom

---

42   The island of Trinidad was a British colony headed by a monarch referred to as 'the Crown', represented at the local level by the Governor General. All free land belonged to the Crown, which could be disseminated to whomever was chosen to receive a grant of land.

43   Appendix VIII (d) Chocolate

44   Besson and Brereton Jul 14, 2019, "Cocoa and the Second Frontier (1870–1920) *The Book of Trinidad*"), Port-of-Spain: Paria Publishing Company Ltd., http://caribbeanhistoryarchives.blogspot.com/2019/07/ Retrieved 2022-01-14.

that occurred between the late 1890s and 1920s. Some of the profits filtered down to the labourers and small producers, many of whom were able to educate their children, who were sent away to private schools in Port-of-Spain and areas like Sangre Grande where such schools existed. The profits of the boom contributed to the growth of the middle class, the general spread of literacy and modernisation.[45]

The early 1920s witnessed a sharp fall in cocoa prices all over the world. The situation worsened in the 1930s when witch-broom disease swept through the cocoa industry, effectively bringing significant cocoa production to a halt. Some migrants drifted off to other parts of the island, mainly to Port-of-Spain.

The Toco Main Road,[46] a major piece of infrastructure undertaken by the government was advancing at the time. From reports it appears that this road was started prior to 1922, and was still under construction when Isaac Arthur arrived. This new road was expected to transform the Region, opening it up to the rest of Trinidad. Running the length of the north-eastern coastline for some thirty-five miles, and ending in Sangre Grande, the road would merge here with the Eastern Main Road, a main east-west artery in the island's transportation system.

The 1930s saw the completion of the Toco Main Road which ended the Region's isolation by land from the rest of the island, and its dependence on the "Round The Island Steamer Service" which had lasted for more than one hundred years. The Road now provided access by land in and out of the region, and villagers could walk or make their way to Sangre Grande to catch the train from where they boarded the eastern branch of the Railway Service to Port-of-Spain, via the Roundabout.

Port-of-Spain markets were now within reach, by land!

---

45   Besson and Brereton Jul 14, 2019 - Cocoa and the Second Frontier (1870–1920) *The Book of Trinidad,* Port-of-Spain: Paria Publishing Company Ltd., http://caribbeanhistoryarchives.blogspot.com/2019/07/ Retrieved 2022-01-14

46   Appendix II (c) (ii) The Toco Main Road

Above:

Passengers boarding one of the Island Steamers. (Paria Archives)

Below:

Detailed Map of Trinidad showing a string of villages running along the North-Eastern coastline of Trinidad.

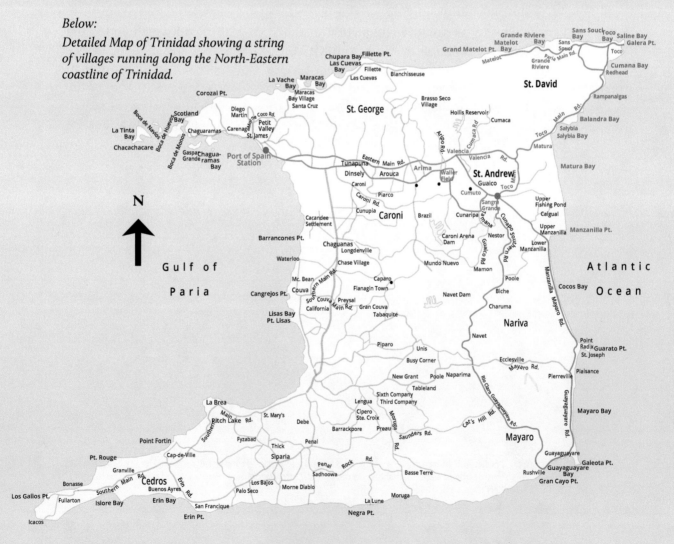

Below:
Detailed Map
of Tobago.

Above:
The Round the Island Steamer. (Paria Archives)

THE

F. G. Alden Co.

EXPORTERS OF

Cocoa,
Cocoanuts,
Copra, and
Balata Gum.

THE F. G. ALDEN CO.,
E. E. Weissenborn,
Attorney.

**PORT-OF-SPAIN,
TRINIDAD.**

Cocoa was such a popular export that images of its likeness were added to postcards and stamps, some of which are shown here.

The F. G. Alden Co. Was one of many exporters of Cocoa, Coconuts, Copra and Balata Gum.

The exportation of Cocoa and many agricultural crops proved profitable for many local businesses.

(Paria Archives)

Above:
A large Cocoa Estate with many cocoa houses. The sliding roof ran on rails, which made it simple to expose the beans to sunshine by opening the roof, or retracting it in the case of a sudden tropical downpour of rain.
(Paria Archives)

Above:
Picking and breaking Cocoa. (Paria Archives)

"Dancing the cocoa."

Right:
A Wooden shovel that was used to scoop up cocoa beans into piles as seen in the photo.
(Paria Archives)

Above:
A few cocoa houses can still be found in Cumana Village and in areas which were once the site of cocoa estates.

Below:

The mortar and pestle was a common household utensil for grinding many food items such as Cocoa and grain. Local Folklore says that the Soucouyant puts her skin in a mortar for safe keeping. (Paria Archives)

PRINCIPAL EXPORTS 1911.

Cacao	lbs.	57,565,088
Coconuts	No.	21,897,031
Coffee	lbs.	40,880
Molasses	gals.	516,284
Coconut Oil	„	1,256
Rice	lbs.	901,743
Bitters	gals.	34,425
Rum	„	122,257
Sugar, produce	Cwt.	758,737
Tobacco, including cigars &c.	lbs.	83,629
Asphalt Crude	tons	134,872
„ Epurée	„	19,283
„ Dried	„	13,320
„ Manjak	„	1,552
„ Liquid	gals.	100
Balata Gum	lbs.	60,432
Timber, produce	c. ft.	110,687
Textiles, value	£	25,159
Hardware „	„	21,017
Oil, Petroleum	gals.	100,707
Bullion and Specie, value	£	14,665

Above:
Trinidad's principal exports in the early 1900s reflect the strength of the agricultural industry at the time.

For nearly three-quarters of a century, the Afro-Franco creole culture, together with its older 'cocoa pagnol' cousinage, boomed. Many small and medium businesses blossomed as a result of exporting cocoa and importing and distributing goods. Many families of the coloured lower and middle classes were able to own small cocoa estates, live comfortably, educate their children, and maintain the values and morals of that respectability so vital in colonial life in those years. In fact, the cocoa boom is what is referred to as the 'good old days', the longtime days of the collective memory of Trinidad as it has come down to us over the years.

(Paria Archives)

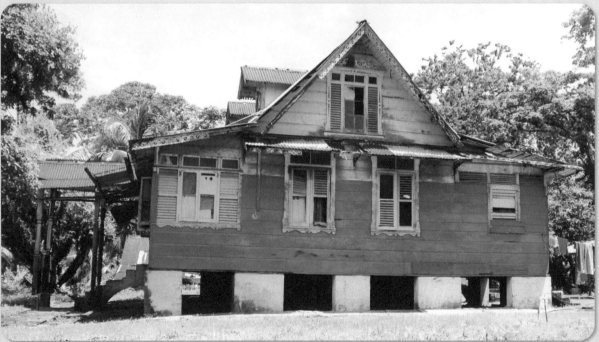

Above:

Features of this Great Estate House on Johnson Hill[47] exemplify an instance of the wealth the cocoa industry created for many in the "good old days". It has a portico entrance with detailed fretwork and a gable roof which was a popular and expensive design feature of the 1900s along with dormer windows.

---

47   Great House on Johnson Hill owned by George Johnson and his wife Ma Johnson during the "cocoa boom, 1870s - 1920s." Last mentioned owner was Bohemia Mariquita Johnson daughter of the Johnsons. Reference. The lady in the attic, the story of Mariquita Johnson. Published on Apr 18, 2017, 12:01 am AST By Richard Charan Multimedia richard.charan@trinidadexpress.com

Above:
The old Port-of-Spain market, where cocoa and other produce were sold locally. (Paria Archives)

Right:
A busy market scene
in Port-of-Spain.
(Paria Archives)

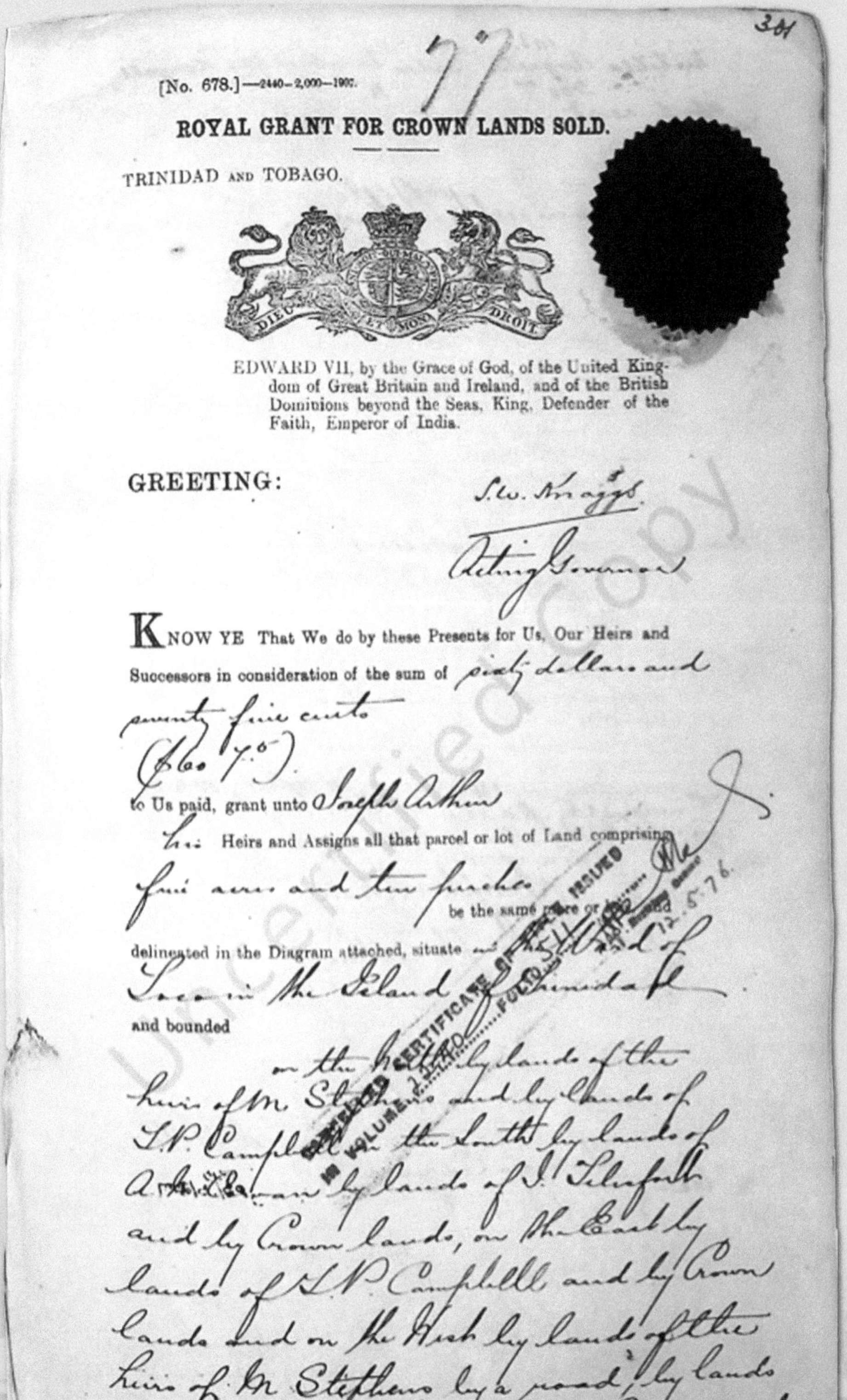
341

77

[No. 678.]—2440–2,000–1907.

ROYAL GRANT FOR CROWN LANDS SOLD.

TRINIDAD AND TOBAGO.

EDWARD VII, by the Grace of God, of the United Kingdom of Great Britain and Ireland, and of the British Dominions beyond the Seas, King, Defender of the Faith, Emperor of India.

GREETING:

S.W. Knaggs.
Acting Governor

KNOW YE That We do by these Presents for Us, Our Heirs and Successors in consideration of the sum of sixty dollars and seventy five cents ($60 75) to Us paid, grant unto Joseph Arthur his Heirs and Assigns all that parcel or lot of Land comprising five acres and ten perches be the same more or less delineated in the Diagram attached, situate in the Ward of Toco in the Island of Trinidad and bounded on the North by lands of the heirs of M. Stephens and by lands of S.P. Campbell on the South by lands of A.N. Cowan by lands of J. Teleufsk and by Crown lands, on the East by lands of S.P. Campbell and by Crown lands and on the West by lands of the heirs of M. Stephens by a road, by lands of P. Cordner by lands of A.N. Cowan and by lands of J. Teleuffsk and intersected by a Road

CERTIFICATE OF TITLE ISSUED IN VOLUME ... FOLIO ... 12.5.76.

Uncertified Copy

Left:
Rare 1929 Crown Grant Joseph Arthur.

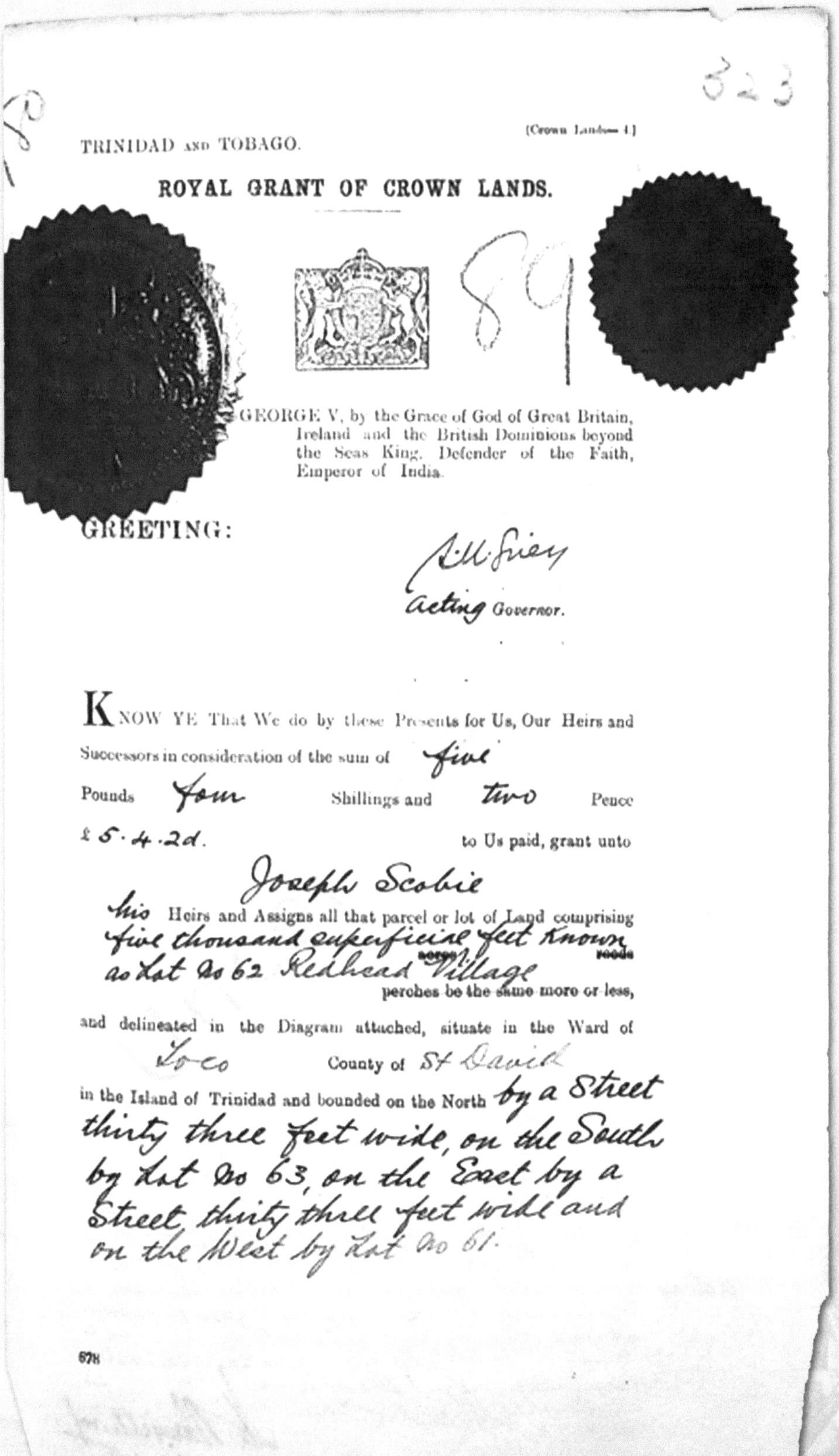

TRINIDAD and TOBAGO.

[Crown Lands—4]

ROYAL GRANT OF CROWN LANDS.

GEORGE V, by the Grace of God of Great Britain, Ireland and the British Dominions beyond the Seas King. Defender of the Faith, Emperor of India.

GREETING:

A.M. Grey
Acting Governor.

KNOW YE That We do by these Presents for Us, Our Heirs and Successors in consideration of the sum of *five* Pounds *four* Shillings and *two* Pence £ *5 . 4 . 2d .* to Us paid, grant unto *Joseph Scobie* *his* Heirs and Assigns all that parcel or lot of Land comprising *five thousand superficial feet known* *as Lot No 62 Redhead Village* perches be the same more or less, and delineated in the Diagram attached, situate in the Ward of *Toco* County of *St David* in the Island of Trinidad and bounded on the North *by a Street thirty three feet wide, on the South by Lot No 63, on the East by a Street thirty three feet wide and on the West by Lot No 61.*

67B

Right:
1934 Crown Grant
Joseph Scobie.

Commanders in 1797 accorded to all those who did not wish to take the oath of allegiance to the King of England to leave the Island, a general census of the inhabitants was taken, of which the following was the result :—

WHITES.

Men.	Women.	Boys.	Girls.	Total.
929	590	301	266	2,086

FREE COLOURED.

| 1,196 | 1,624 | 895 | 751 | 4,466 |

INDIANS.

| 305 | 401 | 190 | 186 | 1,082 |

SLAVES.

| 4,164 | 3,505 | 1,232 | 1,108 | 10,009 |
| 6,594 | 6,120 | 2,618 | 2,311 | 17,643 |

In 1803 the population numbered :—

WHITES.

English	...	...	...	..	663	
Spanish	...	...	...	...	605	
French	...	...	...	...	1,093	
						2,361

FREE COLOURED.

English	...	...	...	...	599	
Spanish	...	...	...	...	1,751	
French	...	...	...	...	2,925	
						5,275
Indians	...	...	...	...	...	1,154
Slaves	...	...	...	...	...	20,464
Total		...		...		29,254

In 1796 the produce of the Island had been :—

From 159 Sugar Estates	...	...	7,800 hhds.
,, 130 Coffee ,,	...	...	330,000 lbs.
,, 60 Cacao ,,	...	...	96,000 ,,
,, 103 Cotton ,,	...	...	224,000 ,,

Census of Trinidad in 1797 and 1803 (35 years before the abolition of slavery) that shows the population at the time split up into races and also indicating free coloured.

The history of chattel slavery is a brutal one, the effects of which can still be seen and felt today.

TRANSITIONS

The change from one state to another

Some of the generation who achieved significant wealth during the cocoa boom sent their children away to private schools in Port-of-Spain and Sangre Grande where such schools existed, or to learn a trade. The 1930s and 1940s, marked the beginning of movement away from the agrarian economy in sections of the Toco Region, to more urbanised pursuits in other parts of the island. The hamlets were expanding, and interest in agriculture was not a priority for the children of labourers who shunned manual labour, the means by which their parents afforded the step up in life for them. The waning agrarian economy was maintained by some who never left.

Although exposure to education was limited to the three R's,[48] there were some fortunate ones who had the means to pursue further education. There is the instance of Albert, the son of Joseph Arthur, Isaac's brother and the proprietor of several acres of coconut trees along the Cumana coastline. Albert, attended St. Mary's College,[49] one the oldest, most prestigious schools in Trinidad. He went on to study law, but unfortunately died at a young age.

Another unfortunate case was that of Sarah who did not get a chance to complete secondary schooling, though for entirely different reasons. She was the daughter of George, Isaac's older brother. At that time, women rarely sought higher education. They could go into manual labour, or become successful proprietors of small business concerns. Some, considered fortunate, got married and became housewives. One exception in the Arthur family was Sarah. It appears that George sent all of his children to school, regardless of gender.

Sarah was described as a tall, brown-skinned goodlooking young lady. She was sent to Dasent High School,[50] the only high school in Sangre Grande at the time. While attending Dasent, she boarded at her Uncle Isaac's home at Rampanalgas to shorten the travelling distance to Sangre Grande from Toco

---

48   Appendix IX (b) 3R's
49   Appendix IX (i) St. Mary's College
50   Appendix IX (f) Dasent High School

where her parents lived. When still a student, Sarah became pregnant and had a daughter. She suffered a nervous breakdown and was committed to St. Ann's Mental Hospital.[51] On her release from St. Ann's, Sarah's older brother Sydney took her into his home where she remained until her death. Relatives do not know or would not name the child's father.

The male relatives who left Toco were mainly tradesmen. There was Cousin Sydney, the one who cared for his sister Sarah after her breakdown. Cousin Sydney was a tailor. He was one of the visitors to our home when I was a child. I had been told that he loved to drink, which I found to be a not uncommon trait among Arthur men, and seemingly taken to the level of sport among quite a few of my countrymen. Cousin Sydney lived in the planning, a government low-income tenement in the East Dry River area of Port-of-Spain. When the planning was destroyed by fire, he moved close to the Port-of-Spain market on George Street which was the infamous red-light district in the city. I was told, "Sydney hung around the market area." Quite likely he knew vendors from Toco who had stalls there, although he might have had other reasons to frequent the area. Later on, he moved to his own private home at Barataria, just outside of Port-of-Spain.

James, Sydney's brother, was a shoemaker. He had a rental store near the jail on Frederick Street. When Cousin Lee spoke of him she made a point of mentioning his association with Miss Dandy. The smile on her face when she mentioned Miss Dandy led me to believe there was more to this relationship which she was either unable or unwilling to recall. Cecil, another brother, became a policeman, and relocated to South Trinidad. Dudley, the second to last brother was a *tunkey*, a prisons officer at the jail on Frederick Street; and Richard, the last brother, was a shoemaker.

Isaac's second eldest brother, Nelson, was a butcher. His sons, Tim Leopold, Neville, and William worked for Gordon Grant.[52] Later Tim and Neville became contractors and formed Arthur Brothers[53], a construction company which was awarded many lucrative Government contracts. They were instrumental in building the Port-of-Spain Town Hall, a wing of the Port-of-Spain General Hospital, and the Salvatori Building, as well as other major construction projects in and around Trinidad, Tobago and the Eastern Caribbean.

Cousin Sim, Simeon Baptiste, the son of Isaac's sister Annie, was also a tailor. He was the owner of a tailoring shop, and a small store front in Cumana. The storefront I believe was the original shop owned by Isaac Arthur which he had passed on to his sister Annie. She in turn left it to her only child Simeon,

---

51   St. Ann's Mental Hospital, Port-of-Spain, Trinidad

52   Gordon Grant was one of the leading business houses in the country with a range of operations under its management including sugar estates and factories...the ownership and operation of cocoa, coffee and coconut estates. gordongrant.com

53   In the 1960s, Arthur Brothers, Neville and Tim Arthur, sons of Nelson Arthur, owned and operated a construction company in Port-of-Spain. They received government contracts including one to build City Hall, in Port-of-Spain. The company later became known as Arthur & DeFour Associates, as they expanded their business throughout the Eastern Caribbean.

a skilled pianist with two supernumeraries. I remember Cousin Sim visiting our house when I was a child. I used to watch, spellbound, as his fat fingers and the two extra ones tinkled away on the piano. I was told that Cousin Sim died suddenly.

Edward, Isaac's nephew and Alpheus' eldest brother, came by his training as a carpenter, through unenviable circumstances. He used this training as the starting point to later become a master carpenter, an advanced woodworker possessing the skills needed to perform any task related to carpentry. It is unknown how Joseph, his second brother, became a carpenter.

Isaac's son Samuel, a much younger cousin of Alpheus, started as a temporary worker at the Telephone Company, and became a permanent worker two years later. He migrated to Canada in the early 1970s. Septie, his brother, worked with Arthur Brothers where he honed his skills, specialising in stone walls. He also migrated to the United States.

More contemporary instances share the thread of unfinished business, all due to unexpected passings.

There is Esmond Scobie (December 29 1936–October 19, 1964), the son of Edward Scobie, Alpheus' brother. He attended the prestigious Presentation College[54] in San Fernando where he excelled at both sports and academics, attaining a scholarship to The University of British Columbia, Vancouver, Canada. Like Albert Arthur, he too died early while pursuing a career in engineering.

'Linroy' L.A.Roy Scobie (September 19, 1948–February 25, 2014) a 'day boarder' of my mother's, was the grandson of Emelda Scobie, Alpheus' sister. He joined the Trinidad and Tobago Police Service but later migrated to Ontario, Canada where he became a member of the Royal Canadian Mounted Police, serving with distinction. He passed away within months of an unexpected terminal diagnosis.

Dr. Dawn AT Phillip (May 23, 1965–October 28, 2017), the granddaughter of Amelia Phillip, Alpheus' sister, attended the University of The West Indies (UWI), St. Augustine and the University of St. Andrews, Scotland. Dawn earned a PhD in Ecology, and lectured at UWI, Department of Life Sciences, a job complementary to her avid conservation sensibilities. Some of her efforts to preserve Grande L'anse Bay, Toco, its environs, habitats for nesting leatherback turtles and the coral reefs are documented.[55] She unexpectedly died, way too young.

---

54   Appendix IX (j) Presentation College, San Fernando

55   Meredith, Mark, "Toco's Turning Tide Part III" Sunday Express, 19 May 2019, p.4. Referencing study by Dr Stanton Belford (USA) and Dr Dawn Phillip of The UWI. "Grande L'Anse Reef...a nesting site for turtles and a source of recreation for Toco residents. Critics say it will be destroyed by dredging and altered coastal dynamics."

Above:
St. Mary's College (CIC) Southern Wing. Albert would have walked through those doors to attend classes. (Paria Archives)

Left:
St. Mary's College (CIC) with students in the court yard. (Paria Archives)

Above:
Roadside vending in Port-of-Spain made it possible for many people from the "country"
to sell their produce in town.

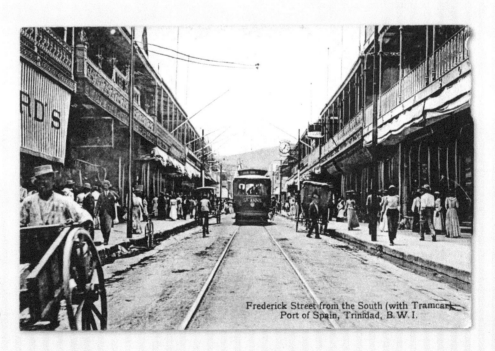

Right:
A busy Frederick
Street looking north.
(Paria Archives)

Above:

Esmond Scobie
(December 29, 1936–October 19, 1964)

An Illustrated Guide to the Freashwater Fishes of Trinidad and Toabgo

Dawn A. T. Phillip
+
Indar W. Ramnirine

April 2001

Above:
Dr. Dawn A.T. Phillip
(May 23, 1965–October 28, 2017)

Above:
'Linroy' L.A.Roy Scobie
(September 19, 1948–February 25, 2014)

THE ORAL TRADITION

Just as my mother told me stories of her predecessors, she was told stories by her mother. Then there are those relatives, if one is fortunate to meet them, who add to the stories, different versions or entirely new ones. The tradition of storytelling is so much a part of how we socialise that sometimes we forget that it is a ritual way of preserving our history. Some relatives have formalised the storytelling by hosting family reunions, a venue to repeat old stories and add new ones. I was able to authenticate some of these stories, and add details using accounts of older relatives, public records and other historical documents.

Margaret

In 2009, the stories of Margaret, her children and her grandson Peter were repeated during a family reunion[56] hosted by Arthur, Cordner, and Saunders descendants. Those stories are some I have documented here.

The family matriarch Margaret had three children by her owner, Arthur Cord(i)ner, two sons and a daughter Ann. The boys, whose names are unknown, were older than their sister who was said to be born *"sometime around Emancipation."* As the story goes before returning to England with their two sons, Arthur Cord(i)ner was said to have given Margaret a handkerchief of coins. Margaret was so distraught at the rending of her family that to prevent her sons from being taken away, she got hold of one son and bit into his ear. Her son's ear was almost severed as he was dragged away from her. It was said that when her boys became adults, they returned to Tobago to see their mother. There was no further information about Margaret.

While searching for documentary evidence of formerly enslaved ancestors, I looked at records released by the British Government in 2009.[57] The 1819 Annual

---

56   Appendix VI (a)

57   All Slave Registers of former British Colonial Dependencies, 1813–1834. The National Archives of the UK; Kew, Surrey, England; Collection: Office of Registry of Colonial Slaves and Slave Compensation Commission: Records.

Return of Unattached Slaves for Arthur Cord(i)ner, described the record of a person I believed to be Margaret, our family matriarch, and her owner. The 1819 record describes a twenty-two year old, black female, Margaret, owned by Arthur Cord(i)ner. Even though the demographic information is bare, her age at the time suggests that she was born in 1797, a time when the importation of slaves to British Colonies including Tobago was unhindered. Cord(i)ner, spelt with an (i), is a variant spelling of the name Cordner,[58] similar to the name of my ancestors and relatives. No other records with similar combinations of owner and enslaved names were found.

Arthur Cord(i)ner, a British subject, the owner of enslaved persons on the Island of Tobago, returned to Europe during the Emancipation period, possibly to England, Ireland or Scotland which were a part of the British Empire. The date of his departure is uncertain. It could have been shortly after the Emancipation Proclamation in 1834, or after the end of the Apprenticeship period in 1838. What is more certain is that Arthur Cordiner would have received a share of the twenty-million pounds sterling paid to slave owners to ameliorate their losses.

I was aware that my ancestors for the most part belonged to the Anglican Church. I also knew that Church records are a primary source of genealogy information, which is why I went to the St. Andrews Anglican Church, Scarborough, Tobago to find Birth, Marriage and Death records of ancestors. While looking, I unearthed a burial record[59] for Anna Cordner of Lambeau, Tobago, date of death, December 19, 1901, age 68 years. I was ecstatic! What this date of death meant was that Anna was born in 1833, the "sometime around the Emancipation period," mentioned in the family oral history! I was sure I had found Ann, (short name for Anna) Margaret's daughter. The name, presumed date of birth, and residence at death, corresponded with those repeated in stories of the Cordners from Lambeau, Tobago. Even though an (a) was added to Ann, I felt confident that I had found Margaret's daughter, Anna.

Anna Cordner of Lambeau, Tobago, was mulatto. Born sometime in 1833, Anna was presumably a member in good standing at the St. Andrews Anglican Church, Scarborough, Tobago. The record shows that she lived at Lambeau and was 68 years old at the time of her death in 1901. She may have even been interred at the churchyard cemetery. I tried to ascertain this, but gave up due to the state of badly damaged tombstones at the cemetery.

Anna had three children: the boy Peter, and two girls, Harriet and Rebecca. Although their father was unknown, it appears that he could have been white

---

58   Cordner is a name for a maker or purveyor of cord or ribbon. Spelling variations are a sign of Anglo Norman names most of which evolved during the 11th and 12th Century. At that time the Norman French language was introduced to a country where Old and Middle English had no spelling rules. Mediaeval scribes spelled words according to sound, so names frequently appeared differently in the various documents in which they were recorded. Cord(i)ner is one such variation of the spelling of Cordner. https://www.houseofnames.com/cordner-family-crest

59   The 1865–1886 Register of Burials in the Parish of St. Andrew & St. George, Tobago. Burial Register, St. Andrews Anglican Church, Scarborough, Tobago. Anna Cordner, L'Ambeau, 1901 Dec. 19, 68 years.

which might explain Peter and Harriet's high brown colour, and Rebecca's very pale skin. Cousin Lee said, "My mother was named after grandma Harriet's sister Rebecca, whose pet name was 'Apple.' Her face flushed bright red, at any hint of emotion. It was said that she was light-headed."

Peter Cordner

Peter Cordner was born in 1854. This makes him twelve years old in 1866, the age at which he is said to have first travelled to the North coast of Trinidad to find work, earning him the designation of 'family pioneer.' Twenty-one years later in 1887, Peter migrated to Cumana Village, Toco. The circumstances of Peter's becoming the family breadwinner is unknown, but from an early age he shouldered the responsibilities that went along with the role. In post-Emancipation Tobago a twelve year old boy would have found it difficult to compete with seasoned adults for scarce jobs on the island. Peter seized the opportunity like other Tobagonians before him to travel back and forth to the north-coast of Trinidad to find familiar work in an unfamiliar location. Initial trips were risky and dangerous, but he braved the seas travelling by the small sailboats used to navigate the treacherous waters where the Caribbean Sea meets the Atlantic Ocean.

Peter must have recognised the potential of the region where he could build a new life and raise a family, not only for himself, but also his sisters, their children, and the wider reach of extended family members. He settled permanently in Redhead, Cumana in 1887 after marrying Catherine Elliott of Lambeau, Tobago. They first lived at Anglais, then moved to the more convenient Redhead Village. He and his wife Catherine had nine children, four boys: Edward, James, Peter (jr.) and Isaac who married Eldica Abraham, and five girls: Ernestine who married Wilson Stafford, Lucy who married Charles Wheeler, Ann, Edith and Ethel. Harriett and Rebecca, his sisters, later joined him. Their children who were born at Lambeau came to the Toco Region of Trinidad at different times. The family's migration to Trinidad did not all happen in one, two or three trips, but evolved over a period of years into a full-blown family migration.

Joseph Arthur and Harriet

Sometime after Emancipation, Joseph Arthur[60], formerly enslaved on the Island of Barbados, a British possession, migrated to Tobago. I had never heard of him, but it was plausible because I knew of Joseph Arthur who turned out to be his son. The senior Joseph proved to be one of the more intriguing ancestors I unexpectedly chanced upon. First documented on the Corbin Estate, St. Peter, Barbados, as a baby slave with both a first name and

60   Appendix VII

surname which did not include any part of his owner's name. Curious? He was freed during Emancipation in 1838. Sometime thereafter he migrated to Tobago, where he settled.

In Tobago, Joseph Arthur joined the rare cast of characters who fought back. He was one of two ringleaders named in a plot to burn and pillage the town of Scarborough. I was surprised at this piece of information, so enlightening to me, so casually presented in a book[61] I had read earlier. I read and re-read the words a few times.

The coincidence was remarkable, I had found baby Joseph Arthur at St. Peter, Barbados in one set of records, and now I was finding him as a grown man, the insurrectionist in Tobago! The immediate cause of the plot is unknown, but in an atmosphere where the natural jubilation following Emancipation had almost worn off, what remained was a thin veneer of civility. This masked the growing resentment at former owners who were devising ploys and legal restrictions to get the formerly enslaved to work for little or nothing on their estates. The citizens fought back in various ways, and I can only imagine that this was his way.

Joseph Arthur was pardoned in 1858 following four years of confinement. He was thereafter described as 'a model citizen' of Tobago. I imagine that on his release, he was clever enough to fall back on proficiencies he acquired while enslaved. These appeared to include culinary skills he learned while preparing meals and baked goods to go along with 'teatime' for his English master. He prepared food and baked goods which he sold for a living. Peter Cordner's younger sister Harriett married Joseph Arthur, a man with a past of which her family might have been unaware. Joseph was more than thirty years her senior when they got married around 1875; she most likely was twenty-one years old to his fifty-five years. They had seven children, four boys and three girls: George, Nelson, Annie, Rebecca, Diana, Joseph Jr, and Isaac. Joseph continued to utilise his skills to maintain himself and his young family. After the birth of his son Isaac around 1883, the still sprightly Joseph, now 83 years old and his young wife Harriet had two more children: Mary, my grandmother, and Colonel.

Between 1887, the year Peter Cordner settled in Redhead, and the first quarter of the 1900s, there is no further information about Joseph Arthur in either Tobago or his presence at Redhead, Cumana Village. Harriet must have continued to live at Lambeau, at least until sometime after 1910, the year Alpheus, the last of Mary's five babies, was born. Mary would have been at her mother's home in Tobago for her confinement and childbirth, which was the way of doing things at that time. Soon after the birth of Alpheus in 1910, Mary went to Redhead, Cumana Village.

---

61   Archibald, D. (2003). Tobago "Melancholy Isle" Volume III 1807–1898.

Rebecca Saunders

Apart from what I had been told of Rebecca, the last daughter of Anna Cordner by Cousin Lee; that she married a Saunders and had seven children: Charlie, Daniel, Margaret, Sally, Simon, Martha and Jestina, there was little more information about her. Others who had known Rebecca were long gone. In 2010, I met Doreen Murrell[62], Rebecca's great-granddaughter, the granddaughter of Simon Saunders, in London. Doreen shared that she had been sent as a teenager to London by her grandfather Simon, at whose home she lived while in Trinidad. She was unable to contribute much to her family's history beyond names and dates for the Family Tree. She shared that she had younger twin sisters, one of whom also lived in London with her husband and family; she suffered from debilitating psychiatric challenges. The other twin had committed suicide as a teenager.

My Grandmother Mary

I was able to piece together information surrounding Mary's circumstances, from the generous memories of relatives like Paul Phillip whom I got the chance to speak with. Mary Arthur, the last daughter of Joseph and Harriet Arthur, shared a close resemblance to older sisters Annie and Diana. She was a tall, slender young lady, of light-brown complexion, with long silky black plaits which reached down to her waist. She would have had a comfortable life at home with her parents as the last of four daughters, with four older brothers, and one younger. She was no older than seventeen years in 1902 when her parents gave their consent and she married James Robinson Scobie of Lambeau, Tobago, an older man who may have shaved years off his age (Discrepancies later showed up on his son's birth certificate). She was the opposite of her husband in physical appearance; James was a person of small stature and dark-skinned, a complexion similar to their sons.

Mary got married before her older sister Rebecca did, and it is not clear if other older sisters Annie and Diana were already married at the time. It was unusual for a younger daughter to precede an older sister in marriage in a society shaped by Victorian norms, especially in matters relating to the conduct of proper young women. Parents were formally asked for their daughter's hand in marriage, usually by letter. The suitor received a formal response from the parents who tried to ensure that marriage was to a man of means who could provide for their daughter. Parents did not allow a younger daughter to marry before older sisters except in unusual circumstances.

James Scobie may well have been brought up comfortably as an only child. His father was named as the beneficiary to a sizable sum of money.[63]

---

62   Appendix VI (b) Doreen Murrell Saunders (May 2, 1937–January 24, 2015) was the granddaughter of Simon Saunders, Rebecca Saunders' son.

63   1856 Will of Robinson Scobie, father of James Scobie.

James owned property and a few head of cattle, he was a skilled carpenter and had a good job with the local government. James and his wife Mary had five children: Edward, Emelda, Amelia, Joseph and Alpheus, all of whom were born in Lambeau, Tobago.

The family returned to Cumana from Lambeau shortly after Mary had her baby, Alpheus. One morning, soon after their return, Mary got up, left her sleeping baby and calmly walked down to the beach where she slipped into the warm, indifferent water of the Caribbean Sea and began swimming north towards Tobago. Mary was said to be a strong swimmer and was well on her way to the island which is a distance of some twenty-two miles away. When the news reached her brothers who were also strong swimmers, they were able to swim out, find Mary, and bring her back. Soon after this incident, Mary was committed to the St. Ann's Mental Hospital in Port-of-Spain.

No 15.   SALINE RIVER, TRINIDAD, B.W.I.

Left:
A postcard of Saline River, Trinidad.

Right:
The warm indifferent waters of the Caribbean Seas.

Peter Cordner and wife Catherine Elliott

James Cordner, son of Peter Cordner

1958 Miss St. David, Catherine Arthur, great-
granddaughter of Joseph Arthur, Sr.

Edith Cordner, daughter of Peter Cordner

Barbara Cordner, granddaughter of
Peter Cordner

Ann Cordner, daughter of Peter Cordner

Joseph Arthur jr. (Son of Joseph Arthur Sr.) and wife Phillipa

Colonel Arthur, son of Joseph Arthur Sr.

ALPHEUS' COUSINS

I n 1971 when I first met Cousin Lee, I was a teenager preparing for A-Level examinations.[64] I happened to be at home on the day she visited. Daddy and I were the only ones at home because my mother had travelled abroad to visit one of her friends. I was struck by the looks of this very slender, pale skinned, and well dressed lady. She was about 5' 5" tall, with the greenest eyes I had ever seen, except maybe for those of my childhood friend Kara. Her voice was soft, the prelude to a very gentle demeanour.

Leyonce James

She introduced herself to me, *"I'm Victoria James, your father Alpheus' cousin."* I found it intriguing[65] that my very dark father had such a light skinned cousin. And with those green eyes!

By now I was used to Daddy's various relatives visiting, which was always a treat for me. But who was this one? I knew that his relatives were an interesting array of looks and colours, but none as pale as this one, Victoria. Collecting a thought, she continued, *"Tell your father it's Leyonce, Cousin Lee."*

In 2009, I reconnected with Cousin Lee who now lived in Boston, Massachusetts. By this time I had been living and working in New York for more than twenty years. Cousin Lee had spent several years working at a hospital in Boston and was now retired. I mentioned my interest in meeting relatives who might fill in some of the gaps on our family tree, which was when she said, *"You should talk to your cousins, the Arthur men,"* with a knowing smile.

"Who are they?" I asked. *"Your very tall, handsome cousins. They have a reputation in Toco."*

"Yes? What is their reputation?"

---

64 Appendix XI (d) A-level examinations.

65 I later learned that Cousin Lee had *'gone down the Main'* to Venezuela, as a young woman, where she spent many years before returning to Trinidad. On her return, she migrated to the United States. Somehow Cousin Lee never shared this experience with me, during our many conversations. It would have been insightful for me to learn of her experiences in Venezuela during the 1950s when quite a few Trinidadians went to Venezuela to seek work. When I first met her, most likely it was during her return from Venezuela.

Cousin Lee giggled, while ignoring my question, a sure sign to me that there was more to her comment. I mentioned that I had heard of Joe Arthur, and that Daddy has a cousin James Arthur in Sangre Grande.

"Yes, Joe is one of the brothers, and there is Uncle Isaac."

The name Isaac sounded familiar, but I couldn't be sure.

"Yes, he owned the shop in Balandra, I believe it is still there, just before you get to Cumana... He is my mother and your grandmother's brother. I believe his children still run the shop."

Really? I never saw them at our home in Sangre Grande.

Cousin Lee, it turns out, had attended primary school at Cumana Village, Toco, with Samuel and Septie, two of her Uncle Isaac's sons. She did not know where they lived, but she knew that they were around somewhere. I promised to try to locate them.

It was during one of my visits to Cousin Lee that she told me about her mother, Aunt Becca. *"Mama was young and not yet married when she took your father Alpheus as a baby and cared for him. Some say she treated him as if he was her own child."*

This was news to me. I had been told that shortly after my father's birth, his mother Mary had suffered a breakdown and was committed to St. Ann's Mental Hospital where she died. I thought: I had never even stopped to think of who took care of my father as a newborn baby, I just assumed that his father did. Puzzled and surprised by what I had just heard, I stared intently at Cousin Lee. I noticed that her aged eyes, a dull green, now seemed more grey than green as she gazed into the distance, her drawn face a picture of wistfulness. She went on to relate, *"Mama had a real soft spot for your daddy, and we all looked up to him as a big brother."* She laughed as she recalled, *"Cousin Alpheus kept us children straight!"*

I shook my head and smiled. I got to thinking about whether Aunt Becca had ever shared any details of Mary's breakdown with her daughter. I questioned Cousin Lee, but she did not know the details of Mary's story. Mary's crisis had occurred in 1910 when my father was born, Cousin Lee was born ten years later in 1920. Back then, adults did not share more information than that which was considered necessary with children, which was very little if any. This practice of selective sharing, would have been even more so at that time, especially when the taint and fallout surrounding the stigma of mental illness, had more far-reaching negative effects, compared to today.

Cousin Lee left me with more questions than answers. I now wished to know even more about Mary. She set in motion my search for Mary. Whatever happened to Mary? How did she die? How old was she when she died? I thought it best to have a chat with my cousin Paul Phillip, Daddy's nephew, the most accessible of my cousins. He was close to his mother, Auntie Amelia who shared many stories with him, stories she had heard as a young lady and some of her own. My chat with Paul would have to wait until I visited him in Trinidad.

Between 2011 and 2013 I continued my visits to Cousin Lee in Queens, New York, where she now resided at the home of her niece; her ageing made it difficult for her to live on her own. During one of my visits, I gained more insight into the closeness and love Aunt Becca had for her nephew Alpheus when one of Aunt Becca's granddaughters who grew up with her recalled Alpheus visiting their home. She recalled, "Grandma, and this cousin Alpheus would pull chairs together, sit down, and talk *'hush, hush'* to each other about their own business. We children were not included, and wondered among ourselves, who is this Alpheus cousin with this funny name? And she, grandma, saved the best for him too. She saved the biggest mango or avocado, whatever she had for when he visited."

This recollection of my father prompted me to inquire about his elder brother, Joseph. Cousin Lee's silence and her hesitant, sheepish smile made me feel disinclined to pursue the subject any further. I felt I would be dredging up what she might have witnessed as abusive and unjustified behaviours by relatives who shunned Joseph, because of his dark skin colour, which ironically was no different from that of his brother Alpheus. In addition his large, broad nose might have been viewed by some as unattractive. Uncle Joe's daughter Eunice told me, "Daddy said they called him Blackbird when he was a boy."

Rufus Stafford

In August 2010, I met Rufus Stafford,[66] a relative who knew my grandfather, James Scobie. Despite being a much younger man, Rufus claimed to be friendly with the older Scobie. I asked him to describe my grandfather so that I could have a picture of what he looked like in my mind. Rufus said that Mr. Scobie was a small, dark-skinned man, about the same height as he, about five feet, four inches. Normally a taciturn and withdrawn person, he did not seem to mind chatting with Rufus whose shared diminutive stature may have been a reason for bonding.

James Scobie had a good government job with the County Council, and owned property in the village, as well as a few head of cattle. He owned a bicycle which looked bigger than he did when he rode by on his way to work. He was one of the few persons who worked on blasting the site for the Tompire Bridge, a major connective link along the Toco Main Road. This explains why years after completion of the job, his second son, Joseph, lost three fingers while playing with dynamite found in his father's toolbox.

---

66   Appendix VI (b) Rufus Stafford, aka 'Cap' 'Hero' 4/9/1926–12/28/2010, was the son of Ernestine Stafford née Cordner, and the grandson of Peter Cordner. He was a second cousin to my father Alpheus Scobie.

Rufus helped me to fill many gaps in our family tree because he seemed to know most if not all of the relatives who lived in Cumana Village. Even though he did not have much information when I questioned him about James's wife, Mary, he knew that, *"Mr. Scobie liked the ladies,"* going on to comically describe a relationship my grandfather had with a one-legged villager.

Paul Phillip (nephew)

In 2014, I visited my cousin Paul Phillip, Daddy's nephew in Trinidad. Together we took a trip to Cumana Village where several relatives still live. While driving northwards on the Toco Main Road, Paul stopped the car just short of a shabby railing running alongside the road. We walked a few feet to where we saw a shallow pool of still water, the bottom clearly visible, the river-mouth—a pool of harmless looking water separated from the sea by a few feet of sand. Pointing to the water Paul said, "Our cousin, Dowling Arthur,[67] a nurse at the St. Ann's Mental Hospital, drowned here in 1982. His car ran off the road and plunged into the river-mouth, he may have fallen asleep at the wheel..." I connected this story to information I gathered from William "Bill" Arthur,[68] another cousin, whom I interviewed during a previous trip to Cumana. While filling gaps on his branch of the family tree, Bill did mention that his brother, Dowling, had died in an accident.

This was when Paul went on to tell me about our grandmother Mary's tragic fate, and about her attempting to swim to Tobago, the story that I related earlier. Paul had heard the story from his mother, Auntie Amelia. Previous to hearing Paul's story about Mary's fate, her story had been shared in a manner that seemed straightforward. "Your father's mother died in St. Ann's after he was born." No frills attached, effectively shutting out further questions. Perplexed even then, I surprisingly left the story alone, at least at that time. I am one of Mary's grand-children, and this is what I had been told.

The story I heard from Paul was chilling, and it made me feel very sad. At first I was shocked at the stark details, then confused, as my mind tried to grapple with what I had heard. My thoughts raced to postpartum 'baby blues,' a period after the birth of a child which can trigger depression and unusual behaviours in a new mother. I realised that the diagnosis I had reasoned is now a commonly recognised phenomenon. Back in 1910, over one hundred years ago, when Mary had her baby, her behaviour would have been interpreted as "mad." It appeared to be fairly routine to commit persons to the mental asylum for any inexplicable display of bizarre behaviour. A life sentence it seemed to me.

---

67   Dowling Arthur (1942–August 19, 1982), son of Henry Arthur and grandson of Cornell Arthur, Isaac's brother.

68   William 'Bill' Merrit Arthur (12 August–December 22, 2020), son of Henry Arthur and grandson of Cornell Arthur, Isaac's brother. He was the brother of Dowling Arthur.

Even though many years later, and I now had more details of Mary's story, it was still very upsetting to hear of what I imagined as my grandmother's life sentence to the St. Ann's Mental Hospital. I was left to speculate about her end. Mary was not yet thirty years old when she was committed to St. Ann's. Presumably she was then a physically healthy young woman who could have lived to be sixty, seventy, even eighty years old.

Paul had no additional information when I questioned him following his disclosure. At the time I wondered aloud, did Daddy know this story? How long was Mary at St. Ann's? When did she die? Paul, do you think your mother visited her mother at St. Ann's? Maybe Daddy did too? I thought to myself, *Maybe that is what he and Aunt Becca talked about that was so hush, hush?* I related Paul's story to my mother, but she too was unable to provide any additional details.

James it appears was so distraught and traumatised by the loss of his wife that he was unable to take care of his newborn, along with four other children all under the age of seven. An estimation of the birthdays of the children shows that Alpheus was the youngest of three children, all born in three consecutive, stair-stepping years. Amelia was born in 1908; Joseph in 1909, and Alpheus in 1910. The younger children were placed with relatives, and of course, it was Mary's sister, Rebecca who took the baby. It is uncertain if his brother Joseph was placed with any specific relative, as there was never any information about him being sent to anyone anywhere else. Baby Alpheus's sister, Amelia, was sent to well-off relatives in Tobago. At the time she was 21 months old. Edward and Emelda, the two oldest children, remained with their father, James.

I still wonder about Mary. As attractive as she may have been, why was she allowed to marry before her older sisters? What might have been her unusual circumstance?

Samuel Arthur

In 2011, I had the first of many telephone conversations with Samuel Arthur whom I finally located in Kitchener, Ontario, Canada where he had lived with his family for many years. At the time I was working on my father's maternal ancestry and seeking to find out more about Joseph Arthur, the family patriarch. Sounding cautious at first, Samuel reacted with a loud chuckle, more incredulous than derisive, when I introduced myself to him and voiced my intention to write our family's history. His chuckle reminded me of the response I got from another octogenarian when I told her what I was doing, "Good story for a book, but you can't get the real story!"

Samuel had no clue about his grandfather, the original Joseph Arthur, and he had only a vague recollection when I mentioned my father Alpheus Scobie. He admitted to knowing the name, but was unable to recall much more. He told me that his brother, Septie, lived in New York, and how to get in touch with him. I arranged for Cousin Lee, Septie, and myself to meet, which we eventually did. Cousin Lee had the chance to reconnect with her cousin, a giant of a man whose disposition seemed gentle.

In 2017, I finally met Samuel and we were both happy to finally meet in person. At the lofty height of what looked to me like 6'4," I asked if he was the tallest of his siblings. Responding with a self-deprecating "no," he went on to inform me that all but one of his brothers had surpassed his father's 6"2" height. He gave a low chuckle which caused me to smile: I guess he felt a sense of accomplishment at exceeding his father in any way.

Still ruggedly handsome, his features reflected what seemed to be the genetic inheritance of his father's good looks, but with warm brown-skin and light, hazel eyes. Despite his height, his gait was more that of a person fitting in than that of one standing out. He ascribed his rangy physique to weight loss as a result of illness. His still athletic limbs were now proudly displayed in khaki walking shorts topped by a green tartan plaid linen shirt, with which he wore comfortable leather sandals. Observant and not overly talkative, he exuded a polite reserve which masked his engaging personality when he warmed up to me.

Samuel described his father Issac Arthur, with whom he grew up, as a no-nonsense person whose height underscored an authoritative demeanour which was only intensified when he used his voice to make requests, or bend it to exude charm. He spoke in a precise and emphatic manner, not needing to repeat himself twice to be heard.

From Samuel's description, I gathered that Isaac's appearance was striking. He was a tall, powerful man, about six feet, two inches in height, light brown in complexion with a clean-cut appearance. The surprising, greenish brown colour of his piercing eyes held you in his gaze. His serious expression and steady gaze evoked the feeling in strangers that he should be approached with caution. He was neat to the point of fastidiousness, keeping all facial hair well groomed which accentuated his very white, evenly spaced teeth. His stance was erect and he walked with long, purposeful strides. He appeared to be most relaxed when he *parlayed in Patois,*[69] his choice of language to communicate with older persons when he was a charmer. Then his eyes twinkled mischievously.

Samuel wondered whether his father developed this persona because he was a businessman or whether this was his innate personality. Either way, he believed that his father relished the effect he had on strangers. I thought it remarkable how Samuel's description of his father's demeanour, and my

---

69   Parlayed in Patois—speaking a mixture of French and African dialect. The term parlay conveys an expressive and familiar form of communication. A mixture of French and African dialect was the common form of communication in Spanish Trinidad, following the influx of French immigrants and their African slaves as a result of the 1783 Cedula. The dialect was commonly adopted, even though the owner class spoke French and Spanish. When the British seized Trinidad in 1797, English became the predominant language..

father's, seemed similar. Apart from physical dis-similarities, these were strong, serious, men who managed their affairs with authoritarian precision. They both displayed behaviours which set them apart from others around them.

During conversations with Samuel, I realised that he had never heard of his paternal grandfather Joseph Arthur, enslaved in Barbados, who infamously nurtured the seeds of a riot in Scarborough, Tobago. Not a word about him from his father. Samuel observed that, "It is quite possible that my father did not know his father's story, just like we children were unaware of his."

Samuel had very little recollection of his grandmother, Harriet Arthur, and could not name or number his cousins, far less aunts and uncles. He seemed pensive when he reflected on not knowing much about his father's life before he migrated to Toco, and not having close relationships or even conversations about his relatives, even though he grew up surrounded by them. He recalled an occasion, running into two schoolmates Tony and Vernon, on a visit back home after he had moved to Port-of-Spain. These young men he later found out were Arthurs. Although they did not carry the name, they were his first cousins, the children of an uncle.

I too felt the loss at Samuel's lack of information about his father, but also about his lack of knowledge about our common ancestors, all of whom seemed remarkable people in their unique ways, some hauntingly unforgettable, like Margaret, our matriarch and root, or eyebrow-raising like Joseph Arthur, his grandfather. It is this feeling of loss and an urgent need to recover the past that drove me to search public records and seek out those who were old enough to remember. I was eager to share some of this information with him, and was particularly excited to let him know about the original Joseph Arthur. He did not seem interested in the slave story. I had observed similar responses before, some more direct, questioning me as to why I was digging up all this slave story.

It is clear from Samuel's physical appearance and descriptions of his father and other relatives that these were brown people, of mixed race. Samuel's lack of interest in the slave story might have stemmed from a desire to distance himself from our African ancestors. This attitude was not uncommon in former slave colonies where social status and privilege were assigned by race and its physical manifestations—skin and eye colour, and hair texture. In Samuel's recounting of his father's activities in Toco, Isaac's self-confidence, his fearlessness, and arrogance are striking. I could not but wonder whether these characteristics were born of his self-perception as an almost-white man, born superior to darker men. Or was this just the imprint of his audacious ancestor Joseph Arthur?

Additionally, it appears that when Isaac arrived in Toco he already possessed some capital that went into his business venture. This, combined with his perceived colour superiority, would have made him amenable to the government authorities whom he approached for contracts and community projects.

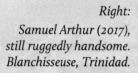

Left:
Victoria Leyonce James
Cousin Lee (2013),
Queens, New York.
Her aged eyes now seemed
more grey than green.

Right:
Samuel Arthur (2017),
still ruggedly handsome.
Blanchisseuse, Trinidad.

REDHEAD

When labourers from Tobago became familiar with the Toco Region, they would settle in areas close to cocoa estates where they worked, and to sources of food, water, and fire. Rivers and streams provided water for domestic use, wooded areas provided lumber to build houses and to make fires for cooking, animals were hunted for meat, and the sea and rivers were good for fishing. Depending on the size of the settlements, some grew into small hamlets or villages, others remained small enclaves of distinctive peoples.

Redhead, a small enclave near to the Allendale Estate[70] this was where Peter Cordner settled with his wife Catherine Elliott in 1877. The area gradually grew into a larger community as his sisters and extended family members joined him. The Arthurs, Scobies and Cordners lived on Back Street,[71] the main thoroughfare, and were among the pioneering families of Wheelers, Staffords, Saunders, and McClatchies who lived in the immediate environs.

Families grew and expanded while some ventured away to other nearby areas like Anglais, Mora, Narang, and Tompire to form new neighbourhoods. Anglais Road became the address of many family members who moved there. Aunt Becca and her sister Annie remained in Redhead while taking care of their ageing mother Harriet, and another sister, Diana McClatchie née Arthur, moved on to Sans Souci *"Big Bay"*, Toco with her family.

Although one cannot be sure, the derivation of some of these curious place names is interesting; Redhead might have been so called because a family in the area had reddish hair. I was told that some of the Arthur and Cordner descendants had very light coloured hair, locally referred to as *'sugarhead.'* The name Redhead stuck to the area which is identified as such on maps today. No one seems to know the origin of the name including relatives who were born and spent most of their lives in Cumana. They describe getting

---

70   Appendix V (a)
71   Appendix V (a)

utility bills reading, 'Redhead, Cumana' as a part of the address, but are unable to connect the name to any local stories. The area may have differed from contiguous hamlets only because of the size of its population which boasted a few more villagers than most of the surrounding communities. Here villagers knew each other and most shared varying degrees of relatedness.

Anglais got its name from the French who named the pathway *Anglais* after the English who forged this path when they first attempted to settle in the area in the 1600s. *Anglais*, the French word for English, is the same path that later connected two Catholic mission estates in the area, one located in Toco and the other in Cumana Village.

The *Narang* area was said to be a virtual orchard of orange trees when the Spanish settled there. The word *Naranjo*, which means orange in Spanish, was localised to *Narang*.

Mora may have been named for the *mora* tree, (also called *matapal*) primarily used for lumber, whose distinctive root system is clearly visible above ground.

When Peter Cordner and extended family members settled in Redhead, they replicated amenities they had access to back in Tobago, and acquired new ones to make their lives comfortable. The men who were labourers, masons, and carpenters were instrumental in building and establishing the St. Ninian Anglican Church and the Seventh Day Adventist Church (SDA) on Back Street (the SDA Church was relocated as the needs of the community grew), and the Anglais Anglican Primary School on Anglais Road. Peter Cordner's son-in-law, Charles Wheeler, became the principal of this primary school which many family members attended, including my father Alpheus Scobie.

The construction of the Toco Main Road, though exciting to villagers, disrupted the lives of those who lived on Back Street when it proceeded on what was described as 'a more direct route' to Toco Village. The new road cut through dense forests, jumped over rivers, rolled into valleys, and bypassed the once busy Back Street which became secondary to this amazing strip of blacktop making its way through unsuspecting hamlets. The bridge and river at the northern end of Back Street disappeared; Redhead and the larger Allendale Estate which was repurposed for residential use, were subsumed into Cumana Village, and the Toco Main Road replaced Back Street as the main thoroughfare.

In 1926, when the Isaac Arthur family disembarked at the Toco fishing depot, following a choppy ride on the high seas, Isaac took his family by donkey-cart to Redhead, Cumana Village, driving along Morne Cabrite Trace,[72] the most convenient and direct route to the village. This pathway may have been more travelled than most, as it seemed clearly defined in some areas, more so than in others where it was assailed by the wild growth of wayward vines

---

72   Appendix V (a)

and prickly shrubbery. The entanglement of undergrowth bursting forth in the humid, tropical heat would have forced Isaac to occasionally dismount to clear an opening for the cart. This journey, I imagine, would have had its own challenges for a pregnant Albertine and two infant children as the cart bounced up and down, sometimes stopping along the uneven pathway.

At Redhead, villagers depended on the steamer service, which in addition to passengers, transported cargo, some of which was earmarked for surrounding villages. When the steamer did not arrive on time, they were forced to forgo necessities and in the case of foodstuff, resort to home-grown crops, fishing and hunting to sustain themselves, at times with limited availability of seasonal produce, or none at all.

Soon after his arrival in the village, Isaac became aware of a void in the availability of staples like flour, sugar, candles, soap, matches, baking soda, other dry goods and sundry necessities between the arrival of one steamer and the next. It was even more distressing to villagers when the steamer was delayed.

Isaac opened a dry goods shop at an accessible location, choosing a spot on the pathway earmarked for the Toco Main Road, and stocking his shop with a variety of staples so that there was an available and dependable source of goods. He gained many customers, but this success was not enough to keep him in Redhead. His family's stay in Cumana turned out to be a short one when he moved on to an even smaller community, Sierra Village where he started another dry goods shop. This venture was short-lived too, for it seems that Isaac had already located the site of his future home, Rampanalgas Village.

Right:
Tompire water treatment plant on the corner of Mora Trace.

Above:
Mora/Matapal Tree. Strong Roots.

Above:
The size of the matapal tree and its roots in relation to the figure standing next to it.

Left:

Mora Forest, Matura, Trinidad. Hamlets of tiny thatch-roofed tapia houses developed alongside country roads. Many of these country roads date from pre-Colombian times and follow the Amerindian footpaths.
(Paria Archives)

Left:
Toco,
Fishing Depot.
(Paria Archives)

Right:
Here huge rock masses rose menacingly out of the sea.

RAMPANALGAS VILLAGE

Isaac Arthur moved to Rampanalgas Village in 1927. At the time he was a forty-six year old man who knew his way around. He was familiar with the region since he had more than likely travelled with his uncle Peter Cordner, older brothers and cousins on trips to work in the area. Starting from a very young age, he had spent most of his life working to take care of his mother and sisters, and later his own family. Now a man of means, he had a vision for his future in Rampanalgas where he chose to make his home.

Isaac's business was thriving when he abruptly handed it over to his sister Annie and left Redhead. This move was incongruent with his normally thoughtful, deliberate and level-headed self. Eyebrows may have been raised at his sudden departure, but he seemed to know what he was doing when he left the small, stifling enclave of close family members. He was father to a very young family, two girls, Jane and Victoria, and now a newborn son, Samuel. Alberta his wife, was especially pleased at Samuel's birth, the first son of her marriage to Isaac who already had one son, Jacob, and two daughters Jestina and Eldica from previous relationships. He did not need his every move to be monitored which he probably felt was happening. His venture into Sierra Village, a smaller community than the one he had just left, where he set up another dry-goods shop, did not seem to be a well calculated move for a man with big dreams. His possible motive could have been to be near to the woman with whom he was carrying on an affair, as his son later mentioned that his father had a daughter with another woman while at Sierra Village.

Rampanalgas Village in the Toco Region is one of the string of tiny hamlets running along the north-eastern coastline of Trinidad. Sometimes loosely referred to as Balandra, it is approximately six miles south of Cumana Village and six miles north of Matura Village. Located just about mid-point on the path of the Toco Main Road which starts at Sangre Grande in the north-east and runs some thirty-five miles along the coast to Toco Village at the northern-most tip of the island. When Isaac moved here, the prospects must have seemed exciting as he imagined the increased flow of people and traffic that would result from the newly built Toco Main Road. This was the perfect place for a shop and rest-stop, as such amenities were few and far between on the path of the advancing road. Travellers would have direct access to his shop located along the path. This traffic would ultimately produce customers for him, which possibilities may have caused him to reconsider his location in Sierra Village.

The name of the village, Rampanalgas, a derivative of the Spanish words, *romper*—to ruin, and *nalgas*—butt cheeks, may have evolved in local parlance as the story of its origin was told and re-told. "A Spanish man while travelling through the area slipped on a muddy path, hombre fell so hard on his backside that he cried out, "Romper nalgas!" The vivid, comic scene and his reflexive response needed no translation. Mimicked in the telling and re-telling, the original Spanish was corrupted, and the cry evolved to one word, Rampanalgas!

Imagine the village when Isaac arrived. A tiny hamlet peeping over the coastline where the white outline of the Toco Main Road was clearly visible, as it forced its way through an area which appeared defeated, relinquishing lost acreage to its gravel path. The Road cut through broad swaths of pristine forest, flanked on the leeward side by tall trees and dense vegetation and on the windward side, thinning forest leading to ridges which edged the land, appearing to be unsupported as they jutted out over the beaches. Here huge rock masses rose menacingly out of the sea, extending to the land, impediments that made passage almost impossible. The severity of the landscape was somewhat relieved by the bays, inlets and serendipitous beaches which held on to the narrow openings allowed by the sea.

Like other villages in the region, Rampanalgas was sparsely populated, undeveloped, with no roads. A bicycle was a rare sight. One got around on foot or by draft animal. Isaac had acquired a donkey soon after he arrived at Cumana Village, which meant he did not have to walk or depend on anyone for transportation. There was no pipe-borne water. The nearest school, church, and cemetery were all located at Matura and Cumana. There was no recreation ground. The mud walls of the tapia huts where villagers lived were at times indistinguishable from the forest as they merged into the curtain of surrounding trees. The fabric of these dwellings, both material and labour, were constructed by teamwork which was vital to keeping the community together.

Depending on the land available, some villagers planted a variety of seasonal crops like cassava, eddoes, yam, tania, potatoes (both plain and sweet-potato), corn, pigeon-peas, peppers, pumpkin, cucumber, tomatoes and okra; several varieties of banana and plantains (*gros-michel, lacatan, bluggoe, chiquito, silk, mataburro* and *zikkia*). Seasonal fruits like citrus—oranges, grapefruit, tangerines, plums and varieties of mangoes, were grown on estates or in backyards. The *tonka* bean which grew in the forest was a peculiar fruit which, if one ate too many, caused a headache. The seeds of the tonka bean were used to make essence, a valuable commercial commodity. Another fruit which grew in the forest, balata, was a small, round, orange coloured fruit which the trees bore every four years. This little fruit was so sweet, it would cause a drunk feeling if too many were eaten. Everyone tended to eat 'too many,' because they were so delicious and rare. The sap from this tree forms a rubbery substance which is also commercially valuable.

Villagers grew sorrel and ginger root which they used to make beverages—in the case of ginger, both hot and cold beverages. Meats and fish were preserved, at times using a boucan, a sturdy wooden frame built to dry meat over a fire, or in the sun. At times salt was rubbed into the meat for preservation. While villagers cultivated crops for their own consumption, they would barter or sell the excess to supplement their income. Apart from yard animals like chickens and ducks, some villagers also reared goats, sheep, cows and pigs.

Food was all natural and organically grown, most of it from kitchen gardens, or it came directly from the sea or forest. Even the animal feed was homegrown. Herbs were grown both for seasoning food and medicinal purposes. Visits to the doctor were rare, partly because doctors were quite a distance away. Most illnesses were diagnosed and treated locally by elders who possessed ancestral knowledge of the most appropriate herbs and potions to treat ailments. Remedies and practises were passed on through generations of families by word of mouth. Lemon grass, also known as fever grass, was boiled to make tea and taken for fever. The aloe plant was used for a wide variety of ailments. *Shadon beni (fitweed), carpenter grass, noni, stinkin'-toe, senna-pod,* and many other herbs and roots were used to treat ailments, some captured in a calypso recalled by Mrs. Cojer-Pritchard[73] describing the saucy conversation between a market vendor and her potential customer:

Man to Woman: *"Ah wat yuh sell dey?"*

Woman to Man: *"Ah minnie-root, ah gully-root, ah johnny-backbone, bitter-sally n' stinkin'-toe, all dat good for young-gal belly."*

At that time there were no funeral homes, refrigeration, undertakers or embalming process as is known today. When someone died, undertaking rituals were performed in the home. Immediate attention was paid to laying out the body: limbs were straightened before rigour set in—hands placed at either side or folded on the chest; a strip of cloth wound from the top of the head and passed under the chin kept jaws closed; big toes were bound together with a strip of cloth, which held the body together; a penny coin was placed on the eyelids when necessary to keep eyelids closed. The recumbent body was left in a cool part of the house or in a makeshift shed built next to the house until such time as the body was *put away. Putting away* meant bathing and dressing the deceased. A family member or an experienced villager saw to the performance of this task. Candles were lit and the house stripped of curtains, a sign to villagers that someone at the house had died, and the family was in mourning.

---

73   Appendix II (b)

The local seamstress was called upon to sew a shroud—burial dress—and the carpenter took measurements of the body to build a coffin. Preservation was minimal, so that burial occurred, sometimes on the same day, or depending on how long the preparations took, not more than two days. Later when ice was handy, it was used for extending preservation of the body.

The Wake,[74] an all-night gathering of family members, friends and villagers at the home of the deceased, was kept going each night before the funeral. Depending on the means of the deceased's family, they prepared food, or got together with villagers who brought food and drinks to the dead-house. Music was provided by drummers, persons with a *shak-shak, grater, tin-cup, tik-tok* and, as the night wore on, anything at hand that could make a noise. Rum, coffee, biscuits and cheese was standard fare, with a pot of *pelau* bubbling on a fire, as villagers milled round, chatting and socialising with each other.

Usually an older villager, or someone who had had more than enough to drink and well into their cups, began the dancing! Others joined in, as the drumming crescendoed, generating lots of excitement as villagers performed the traditional Bongo and Limbo dances. Villagers got a chance to display their skills, as the dancing started with a slight shuffling (chipping), which led to gyrating (wining), then the Limbo, when repeated attempts were made to pass under the progressively lowered bar. The drinking, eating, singing and dancing went on until morning, and was repeated on successive nights as necessary.

After putting away, the recumbent body was laid out in the coffin which was positioned in the open shed erected beside the house for this occasion. Villagers could view the reposed body and pay their respects here. (This outside viewing was gradually moved to the verandah or living room, and eventually to funeral homes and churches.)

At the appointed hour, prayers were said, then pallbearers, friends of the deceased or able-bodied villagers, hoisted the coffin onto their shoulders to bear the body all the way to Cumana village for burial. Pallbearers were rotated at intervals to relieve the burden of carrying the coffin, walking six miles to the burial ground. Years later, when the bicycle became more available, the coffin was placed on the crossbar and the bicycle pushed by pallbearers from Rampanalgas to Cumana.

---

74   The 1962 Calypso, *"Bongo Man,"* sung by The Mighty Wrangler, is a witty and entertaining calypso which hilariously captures the ambience of a Toco wake, and the spirit of the Bongo Dance.

Above:
The Beach, view from Arthur's, Rampanalgas Village.

Above:
The dark jagged rocks of the east coast of Trinidad.

Left:
Draft animal is an animal that has been trained to do work – specifically to pull heavy loads. A cart man making his way through the village as children following behind. A tapia house sits behind the hedge.

Left:
Illustrations of Lemon Grass "Fever Grass" and Shadon beni (fitweed).

Lemon grass is often used to make teas for fever from which it got its nick name..

Shadon beni is widely used in cooking throughout Trinidad and Tobago.

(Paria Archives)

Above:
Aloe plant.

Right:
The picturesque sea scape of the east coast Trinidad.

ISAAC

A man like Isaac would have had little difficulty in negotiating with and recruiting villagers to assist in building the family home. Aside from his charm, he was familiar with traditional practises, growing up as he did in Tobago where *len-hand*,[75] a community effort, was customary. He would have used this knowledge, along with his ability to *parlay in Patois*, to recruit villagers to erect and *lepae*[76] his home.

Isaac usually spoke standard English, but when he parlayed with older villagers he reverted to Patois which made him seem like a different person. He became animated, his facial expression changed, and his eyes twinkled mischievously when he laughed. This was a notably different persona from the one he displayed when dealing with others, during which times he maintained a humorless expression.

The spot Isaac chose to build the family home was on a hillock, a few yards away from the beach and overlooking the path that would become the Toco Main Road. The house was constructed bungalow-style, a few feet above the ground, and was spacious and roomy enough to accommodate his rapidly growing family. There was now a second boy Septimus, followed by a girl named Greta. John, Paul and Grace came later.

The house Isaac built for his family, must have been a far cry from the *tapia* house in which he first lived when he arrived in the village. When it became fashionable to disguise *tapia* with mortar, Isaac upgraded his house. He had the walls of the house plastered with mortar which concealed the *tapia* walls, and gave the house a more finished look. This was a clever way of disguising a mere *tapia* house, a fairly common practice in Port-of-Spain when constructing houses.

The dry-goods shop, a stand alone structure, was erected a few feet away from the family home, where it was easily accessible from within the

---

75   Len-hand - At one time, villagers felt a communal obligation to assist each other. They shared the burden of ventures requiring more than two hands, like building a house.

76   Lepae (pronounced lee-pay) is a highly specialised technique of moulding. See photo on p 80 and Appendix III (a)

village and to travellers passing along the path. This is where Isaac Arthur finally settled.

Hunting Wild Meat

One of Isaac's favourite pastimes was hunting wild meat. Samuel recalled one of the stories his father told them as boys, about the true friendship of Joe Tambe, a villager, which was proved during an unfortunate hunting accident.

One Saturday afternoon in August of 1931, Isaac set off for a hunt with his gun, three dogs, a roasted bake, and a slab of fried codfish, accompanied by his friend and hunting partner, Joe Tambe. After they had gone some distance into the forest, the dogs sighted wild pigs and chased after them. Isaac and Joe chased after the dogs as they chased after the wild pigs. During the chase, Isaac stumbled and tripped over a log, he lost his balance and fell onto a poisonous *mapepire zannana* snake which bit him. Reacting to the sharp pain, he cried out. Joe, who fortunately was behind him at the time, heard his cry of pain and hurriedly ran up to see what had happened. On seeing the snake, Joe immediately shot it and quickly applied an antidote to the wound, knowing that this snake bite could be deadly. Luckily for Isaac, Joe had an antidote in his knapsack, some of which hunters always carried as a precaution. The dogs heard the gunshot, and came back to his side where they lay next to him while Joe returned to the village, some four or five miles away, to seek help.

Isaac described how difficult the trip back to the village was when Joe and a group of volunteers returned with a hammock to bring him home. The men carried his dead weight up and down hillocks, slipping and sliding as they crossed ravines. When they arrived at the village, he was immediately taken by animal another eighteen miles away to the Sangre Grande Hospital where the doctors reassured him that, because of the antidote, he was not going to die from the snake bite.

When he was through with telling the story, Isaac not one to miss an opportunity, seized upon this one to lecture the boys on the importance of having at least one trusted friend, and exhorting, "It is never a good idea to go hunting by yourself, because thanks to my friend Joe Tambe who was with me that day, my life was saved."

Turtles

Turtles are very easily startled and will return to the sea without laying eggs if they sense any disturbance.[77]

Another of Isaac's favourite pastimes was *"hunting turtles"* a subject about which he was very knowledgeable. He could look at the sky, pinpoint certain stars and predict on which beach a turtle would lay her eggs. He could also

---

[77]   The Turtle Trust. Sea turtle conservation. Retrieved December 13, 2020 from turtlevillagetrust.org

look at the eggs and tell whether it was the turtle's first or second laying and how many days later she would return, looking for a safe spot to lay again.

Isaac taught his boys how to hunt turtles. He taught them the procedure: You first look for the turtle's head in the water, and when it appears, keep your eyes fixed on it and remain still as the turtle emerges from the water. You then ease up next to the turtle as she walks on the sand, and walk alongside her for a few steps before reaching down, holding the sides of the shell, and flipping the turtle onto its back with both eyes closed to avoid sand flying into them from the flapping motion of its feet. While still on its back, wash all the sand off the turtle, as it is more difficult to remove after the turtle is killed. The turtle was hunted for its meat, eggs and shell.

Depending on the turtle species, usually the female would carry about forty to fifty eggs which she was about to lay. The eggs, when broken, consisted of a small amount of white or albumen which, unlike the white of hens' eggs, does not congeal. The yolk is plentiful, and Isaac used it to make a delicacy which they named, *malsee*.[78] Villagers were limited to buying two or three eggs each, allowing families to at least have a taste of Isaac's *malsee*.

The flesh of the turtle was extracted from the hard outer shell, cut into pieces and sold to villagers. At that time, almost everyone relished the idea of eating turtle meat and eggs. The meat was seasoned and cooked like any other meat. The shells were washed, cleaned, dried and sold, to meet the demand for turtle shells both locally and overseas. The shells were used to make novelties like guitar picks, hair accessories, and decorative items.

Back then hunting turtles was normal. There were thousands of turtles, a small fraction of which provided a source of food and livelihood for villagers. There was always the expectation that they would return during succeeding seasons. Turtles are now an endangered species.[79] The threats to their existence justify the current prohibitions against hunting them. These conditions did not exist in Isaac's time. Turtle hunting was one of the few pastimes Isaac taught his boys and which they all enjoyed doing together. Isaac found the time to do what he enjoyed best, hunting wild meat, and tracking turtles.

Amenities

When Isaac chose Rampanalgas as the location for his home, it seems that he was motivated and determined to improve the conditions which existed there at the time, knowing that any improvement to the quality of life for villagers would benefit his family as well. Alberta, his wife, like other villagers, cooked on stones, because there were no coal-pots or stoves. When the coal-pot became popular, Isaac replaced the stones with one, and charcoal (coal) was now used instead of firewood.

---

78 Malsee - the yolk was seasoned with spices and stuffed into the small intestine of the turtle to make a sausage-like delicacy which they named malsee, a name local to the village.

79 Laws of Trinidad and Tobago. Fisheries Act. Chapter 67:51. Act ... Protection of Turtle and Turtle Eggs Regulations.

Isaac was concerned that his wife did the family cooking in the open yard while tending to infant children. This setup was inconvenient, especially when it rained. He built her a kitchen, a separate covered structure, behind the main house. He built the clay oven used for cooking inside the kitchen where it was more convenient. With wood and coal being used for fuel, he thought it best to collect a large amount, burn it, and store the coals instead of making frequent trips to the forest to collect small amounts of firewood. He got together with the village men to build a coal pit[80] where they burnt firewood and produced a large quantity of coal. Isaac stored his, while some villagers made money by selling their extras.

There were no schools in Rampanalgas. The nearest ones were at Matura and Cumana. An enterprising villager, Cousin Netta,[81] ran an informal kindergarten at her home. Isaac sent his children to this preschool which his son Samuel attended sometime around the age of four years. When Cousin Netta was no longer able to carry on her kindergarten, Isaac offered to house the preschool in an unused room next to his shop. He paid a new teacher, Mr. Jose Mark,[82] out of his own pocket. He did not solicit contributions from other villagers whose children attended the preschool. It appears that Isaac was very concerned about younger children being deprived of basic education, and did what he could to facilitate their access to learning. He maintained the preschool on his premises, sometimes including older students until the Rampanalgas RC School[83] was built.

The closest cemetery to Rampanalgas village was in Cumana, some six miles away. At that time, villagers carried the coffin on their shoulders in the hot sun, or even worse in the pouring rain, all the way to burial. The introduction of the bicycle to transport the coffin did little to relieve the agony of maneuverability and trepidation at the thought of, God forbid, the coffin falling off the handlebars. Isaac was moved to petition the County Council for land in Rampanalgas to be designated a cemetery. His petition was successful and a parcel of land next to what today is the Rampanalgas RC. School was allocated for that purpose. Villagers could now bury their loved ones close to home. The Rampanalgas Public Cemetery which was referred to by some as *"Innocent Cemetery,"* was reported to have gotten this name because its very first occupant was a still-born baby.

Villagers showed their appreciation by keeping the cemetery well tended. Particular attention was paid to cleaning of grave sites in time for November 1,

---

80 Piles of fallen trees from the forest were collected and sawed into logs roughly eight feet in length. The logs were stacked beside each other in rows of about sixteen feet long and five feet high. The pile was tightly compacted, sealed at the sides and topped with clay, then set afire and left to burn. After a week or so when the logs were completely burnt, the pit was opened, and the residual charcoal (coal) extracted.

81 In the late 1920s and early 1930s, Ms. Anita Theodora Tappin, known to many as "Cousin Netta" operated a semi-formal private school for infants at her home in Rampanalgas village

82 Mr. Jose Mark, was a gentleman paid by Isaac Arthur to teach village children in a room set aside in the family home, after Mrs. was unable to continue her school. Mr. Mark and those who followed him continued the practice until the first school, Rampanalgas R C School, was built in the village.

83 The Catholic Board built the Rampanalgas R C School next to the cemetery, sometime after 1936.

known as All Saints Day, and November 2, known as All Souls Day. Following Christian custom, families lit candles, prayed and placed flowers on the grave sites of departed loved ones.

It was the late 1940s and Isaac's family now included four boys. He needed to find creative ways to keep them and the other young male villagers occupied. Rampanalgas had roads, a dry-goods shop, a cemetery and a school. There was no place for youth to meet and socialise, except for the schoolroom next to the shop, which Isaac permitted but which was not always convenient. Rediffusion[84] service, introduced to the Island, now allowed Trinidadians to listen to cricket. This was especially appreciated by those who could not travel to the Queen's Park Oval in Port-of-Spain where all the important cricket matches took place. It therefore was not farfetched for Isaac to think of cricket, the most popular sport at the time, as a means of keeping the young men of the village busy. It was just the right outlet for them, competitive but a team sport. Isaac put his mind and resources to work, and was instrumental in getting a nearby parcel of land designated as a recreation ground for villagers.

The young men of the village formed a cricket club. The paraphernalia required for the game was expensive, with costs outside the reach of most members. The club came to an arrangement with Isaac where he paid in advance for the cricket gear and was reimbursed for his expenses by club members over a period of time. Members of the club were allowed to continue using the room next to the shop to hold meetings.

Team members prepared the field prior to games, smoothing the pitch, and setting up boundaries. Everyone could not participate, and those who could not were just as enthusiastic as those who did. During games, voices could be heard shouting, *"Hit the ball!" "Six!" "Run man!" "LBW!" "Duuuck!"* Wives, girlfriends, villagers, some from other villages, all came to see the matches and support their teams. The ladies brought baskets of food and drinks, refreshments for those looking on to enjoy, and everyone took the opportunity to socialise. Sometimes the fun was so contagious that even passers-by (the Toco Main Road was open) would stop their cars, spending a few minutes to look on. A well-known passer-by might even be allowed to take a turn with the bat. The grounds saw its fair share of tournaments, as the young men grew more confident, even playing against teams from as far away as Port-of-Spain.

The cricket ground was a great source of pride and joy for Isaac. Yet his contribution to the existence of the recreation ground was ignored when it was named for someone whose influence was peripheral to the initial designation and support of the grounds. It is believed by some villagers that the naming was due to the person's association with one or more of the prominent estate owners in the area.

---

84   Rediffusion (Trinidad) Limited created the Trinidad Broadcasting Company in 1946 which launched Radio Trinidad 730 AM in 1947. https://www.wikiwand.com/en/Radio_in_Trinidad_and_Tobago#/overview January 1, 2022.

Above:
Isaac Arthur - Uncle Isaac "Tall and handsome".

Above:
Tapia house -
Cumana Village.

Left:
Man doing lepae -
filling in the walls
of the Tapia hut,
was done by hand
as seen here.
(Paria Archives)

Above:
Tapia huts/houses can still be found in and around Cumana Village. Some have been outfitted with electricity.

Above:
What Arthur's small coconut estate may have looked like. (Paria Archives)

Above:
The trek to Sangre Grande Police Station by donkey was not easy by any means.
(Paria Archives)

Right:
What the road to the Sangre Grande Hospital would have looked like.
(Paria Archives)

Left:
Donkey/Burro proved useful to help transport produce to and from the market.
(Paria Archives, Fern Mackenzie Collection)

83

Above:

Grand Riviere circa 1920s. Leatherback Turtles have always returned to this location each year to lay their eggs, and continue to do so now. Before the prohibition of hunting turtles, the eggs and meat provided food for villagers, and the prized shells were sold. (Paria Archives)

Hawksbill Turtle   *Green Turtle*   *Leatherback Turtle*

Above:

Illustrations of turtles commonly found in Trinidad and Tobago. (Paria Archives)

Left:

Trinidad is famous for the nesting of Leatherback Turtles in Grande Riviere. Several other species of turtle including the Hawks bill can also be seen feeding and nesting on the East coast of the island.

Salibia Bay, pictured here from the old swing bridge.

(Paria Archives)

Above:
A young man monitors the charcoal pit.
(Paria Archives)

Below:
Illustrations of
"wild meat"

Agouti

Brocket Deer

Lappe

Quenk

Above:
Outdoor clay oven of recent use, fuelled by wood, charcoal and occasionally coconut husks.

Above:

Queen Park Oval during a cricket match with a large crowd of spectators. (Paria Archives)

Above:

Queen Park Oval pavilion. (Paria Archives)

Above:

Two young men sporting "cricket gear" of the time. (Paria Archives)

VILLAGE LIFE
1930S & 1940S

Local Roads

Right:
Postcard depicting
what rural village life
looked like.
(Paria Archives)

The construction of the Toco Main Road was a major project for the island. There were at least three references to it in the Port-of-Spain Gazette,[85] during the months of April, May and June of 1922,[86] all prior to Isaac Arthur's settling in Rampanalgas in 1927.

9 April 1922: "'Candid Comments' expects Toco road to be finished by end of May 1922...There is now only ¾ mile of bridle road, but crossed by deep ravines, etc..." 20 May 1922: "Toco Main Road likely to be finished in six weeks..." 17 June 1922: "Governor expected to open the Toco Main Road for wheel traffic; ... Quite an unusual number of strangers was seen here during the past week, Portuguese and Chinese forming a fair proportion."

---

85   The Port-of-Spain Gazette (POSG) is an official government publication which carries official government in-formation and which is legally required to be published.

86   Craig-James, Susan. *"Notes on the Sangre Grande Courthouse and the Toco Main Road."* See Appendix II (c) (ii)

The articles conveyed the impression that the road was near to completion, but it was not completed until the mid-1930s.

Isaac noticed that the construction of the Toco Main Road did not flow in a continuous pattern, seemingly random sections were completed before others and eventually linked. A small stretch of road running in front of his shop was paved with asphalt to take care of what was described as, "a miserable dust hazard in the dry season, and a mud hole when it rained." It seems that this selective paving might have given Isaac the idea to try to bring some of the construction work from the Main Road to the village where local roads were badly needed. Village men who had worked on paving the front of his shop were quite capable of doing the job and they needed work.

The government was in a phase of Crown Colony rule which the ambitious and resourceful Issac negotiated. Isaac put in his bids to build local roads in the village. Isaac was awarded the contracts to build these secondary roads. This was his first big negotiation with government officials. In his new role as a government contractor, he could provide much-needed jobs for villagers. Isaac hired men whom he knew to be capable, industrious and reliable, and who could do the job. Manual labour was the order of the day. Labourers used pickaxes, cutlasses, hoes, shovels, and even their bare hands to cut paths through the forest. As the forests were cleared and paths cut, they were paved with sand and gravel, a bucket at a time, making them navigable. The wives and girlfriends ably supported their men by providing meals and water as they worked in the hot, blazing sun.

The newly paved pathways brought about much-needed improvements in mapping, defining boundaries, and added stability to former unstable paths. Some of the sand and gravel paths were later paved with asphalt. This road building laid the infrastructure for further development of the village, while enabling the labourers to better provide for themselves and their families. Men worked for thirty-six cents a day, five days a week. Comestibles were cheap then, as one pound of flour was three cents, sugar was four cents, and hops bread was ha-penny (half-penny or one cent).

Under Isaac's watch, roads were built from Langusta Village to Guayamara Village. Duke Street was developed, as well as other village streets which were once wooded parts of the forest.

Breakfast River

A rest-stop where market vendors refreshed themselves, during the long trek from Matelot Village to Sangre Grande.

The opening of the Toco Main Road came with the expectation that vehicular traffic would flow on this route, but that did not happen right away. Vehicular traffic was a rare sight, usually cars belonging to travellers who had business in the region, and these weren't many. The use of draft animals, carts and walking continued to be the most common ways to get from one place to the next. Articles about the Road referenced the transportation available at that time: "The oldest known *'Carter'* in Toco, Darling Barbast, bought a bus licensed for seven passengers for use in Toco."[87] Carting was a recognised form of transport throughout the island, owned or managed by a person known as a *carter*. Prior to the arrival of motorised vehicles and the construction of asphalt paved roads, carts were used for carrying heavy goods and for passenger transportation. The cart retained its usefulness for many years after the Main Road was completed. Private transportation was cost prohibitive for most.

The Public Transport Service Corporation (PTSC),[88] did not come into existence until almost thirty years later in 1965. Until then, villagers from as far away as Matelot Village walked the distance of some forty-five miles to Sangre Grande where they caught the train to Port-of-Spain and the market.

Villagers left home long before daybreak to get to their destinations which most times were the Port-of-Spain markets. There were still no street lights, and the densely forested areas where many of them lived was pitch black. The *flambeau* was used to light the way as they walked. Before leaving home, market vendors took tea, usually made of boiled leaves such as lemon grass, lime leaves, *chandelier bush*, or whichever herb was preferred. This was drunk alongside bakes[89] and codfish when available.

At Guayamara, the vendors stopped just beyond the village at a river located a few yards away from the Catholic nuns' vacation home. It was now time for the second meal of the day, breakfast. Here the vendors ate, drank clean water, and did their ablutions before continuing on the walk to Sangre Grande. This river came to be known as *"Breakfast River."* A little further down, about half-mile to the south of Rampanalgas Village, the owner of Farfan estate, the descendant of an original Spanish settler, built a guest house known as *"The Rest House."* Travellers with means could stop here to rest and even overnight.

It was said that the very first bus to drive along the Toco Main Road was nick-named *"WITHIN THE TIME."* This was confirmed by Mrs. Victoria Cojer-Pritchard of Cumana Village who stated that she was a regular passenger on this bus, commuting to and from Sangre Grande, sometimes catching the train onwards to Port-of-Spain. She recalled waiting at the roadside in Cumana for *"WITHIN THE TIME"* bus which earned its name from its invariable punctuality as it plied between Matelot Village and Sangre Grande. The bus held about fourteen passengers and was privately owned.

---

87   Appendix III (c)

88   The Public Transport Service Corporation, the sole operator of the country's commercial bus service came into being on May 1st, 1965. The PTSC provided a safe, clean and inexpensive transport service for the people of Trinidad and Tobago. https://www.ptsctt.com/history accessed October /3, 2021.

89   Bake - a Trinidad styled round, flat bread made from flour, baking powder, butter and salt with coconut optional. It is kneaded into a soft dough, baked and eaten with cheese or other delicacy.

Riparian Rights

The right to use water as long as such use does not harm upstream or downstream neighbours

It was not long before Isaac became recognised as an upstanding leader in the community. He was, or fancied himself, a law-abiding citizen who was responsible for keeping other villagers in line. He spared no effort in doing so.

Isaac's property, overlooked the main road, and was backed by the homes of other villagers. Just beyond these homes was a river on which the community relied for water to cook, wash clothes and bathe. Water for domestic use was collected upriver where a bridge served as the marker to determine upriver leading back to the source, and downriver which followed the current to the sea. This was a sore point for Isaac who believed that all washing of clothes and bathing should be done downriver to avoid pollution of the upriver water used for domestic purposes and drinking.

One Sunday morning while taking his daily walk along the river-bank, Isaac noticed that the water above the bridge looked soapy as though someone had washed in the river. He walked a little further and noticed Mr. Sammy, one of the villagers, swimming. He became annoyed at Mr. Sammy and confronted him. Mr. Sammy, cheekily admitted to washing his work clothes in the river and informed Isaac that he was now taking a bath.

Incensed at Mr. Sammy's attitude, Isaac got on his donkey and rode all the way to the Toco Police Station where he reported the incident. Unfortunately for him, he was told that even though he had made a complaint, he could not make a case without a witness.

Isaac dropped his complaint against Mr. Sammy, but remained undeterred and adamant about the boundaries for washing at the river. He firmly believed that he was doing his part to ensure that everyone's riparian rights were respected, that the community had clean water, and that everyone was protected from the spread of disease. He addressed issues he believed to be of concern to the community, sometimes along with others and at times taking matters into his own hands as he did on this occasion.

On another occasion, Isaac took a parent to court for using obscene language. A student in Samuel's class was punished by the teacher with two strokes on his buttocks. This was not an unusual form of punishment at the time, but the student complained to his aunt, Mrs. Cecil, about the punishment. Mrs. Cecil came to the school in a rage and *cussed-up* the teacher, using a generous amount of four-letter words in the presence of the class, the teacher, and Samuel. Samuel reported what had happened in class that day to his mother who in turn reported it to Isaac. When Isaac heard of the incident, he mounted his donkey and rode all the way to the Sangre Grande Police Station where he filed a complaint against Mrs. Cecil. A summons was issued for Mrs Cecil to appear in court. Mrs. Norma, the teacher, and Samuel were called as witnesses to Mrs. Cecil's behaviour, to which she pleaded guilty.

This time Isaac did not forget to take witnesses with him! This seemed to vindicate his prior actions, and bolster his insistence on intolerance for lawlessness and indecent behaviour, and that everyone should uphold the law.

Right:
Postcard of children
playing in a river.
(Paria Archives)

River Scene, Trinidad. B.W.I.

Above:
A river scene shows what 'Breakfast River' may have looked like as travellers stopped for a drink of water and a bite to eat.
(Paria Archives)

Left:
Washday at the river was an opportunity to socialise and catch up on the local gossip.
(Paria Archives, Fern Mackenzie Collection)

Above:

The daily activities at the river made up a big part of people's lives. "Blanchisseuse" translated from French means "Laundress," a woman whose employment is laundering clothes.

The village of Blanchisseuse is located about midway along the North coast of Trinidad on the northern slope of the Northern Range. (Paria Archives)

Right:
Two women make their way home on the newly paved road or "the black top" as it was known.
(Paria Archives, Fern Mackenzie Collection)

Above:
Before roads were paved in rural areas of Trinidad, foot paths criss-crossed the country side. (Paria Archives)

Left:
Having a donkey "burro" made life much easier.
(Paria Archives, Fern Mackenzie Collection)

Above:
"Within The Time," the omnibus was one of the ways to get to the Sangre Grande train station.
(Paria Archives, Fern Mackenzie Collection)

DRY GOODS SHOP

A shop that carried items such as candles, matches, sugar, flour, coffee, rice, and salted fish, generally items that do not contain liquid...

I t was the mid-1930s, and the Toco Main Road was completed. Isaac began to see a small increase in foot traffic, carts, and the rare motor vehicle of a traveller who had business in the area. During construction of the main road, labourers had already begun to frequent the shop for small items. Now travellers passing through the village would occasionally stop to buy food and drinks.

Although workers had their meals and beverages taken care of at home, Isaac thought that labourers, particularly the single males, needed an occasional treat—something sweet in their lives. Always the businessman, Isaac set up a little wooden parlour next to the shop where he sold home-made drinks, hops bread, coconut drops and cakes. He loved baking pastries and preparing delicacies, which seemed totally out of character with his unmistakably manly demeanour. The apparent contradiction suggests the influence of the elder Arthur on his son. It is curious that one generation later, Isaac's eldest son Jacob, also displayed baking skills. It is believable that he in turn would have learned these skills from his father as a young child growing up in Tobago.

Isaac enjoyed making hops bread, coconut drops and other pastry-like treats. The coconut drops he made were a favourite with everyone. Samuel recalls, "The mouth-watering smell of those drops baking was only bettered by the taste." Patrons washed the drops down with a glass of cold mauby which cost one cent. The drops cost a penny (two cents).

Isaac also raised pigs which he fed the left-over pulp from processed coconuts. Sometimes he would butcher a pig, use a portion of the meat at home and sell the remainder at the shop. While ensuring that nothing of the pig went to waste, he made black pudding,[90] a sausage-like delicacy from pig's blood. Some of the black pudding was sold at the shop. At home the family ate the black pudding with fresh hops bread.[91]

90   Black pudding is a mixture of pigs' blood, combined with mashed potatoes and lots of fresh seasoning, herbs and peppers. The intestines of the pig are cleaned and the mixture stuffed into it. It is then boiled to ensure that it is thoroughly cooked. After cooling, it is cut into pieces for serving.

91   Hops bread is a Trinidad styled salt bun which has a thin crust on the outside and is puffy, light and chewy on the inside. Its unique consistency is achieved in the kneading. The bread is baked on banana leaves and retains a trace of the leaf flavour.

The shop sometimes served as a recreation centre for villagers. Samuel recalled the time his father held a dance at the shop. He believed it was in the early 1940s. This was a big event for the villagers and those nearby. Isaac loved dancing but did not have many opportunities to do so. On this occasion, he hired a live band all the way from Arima to provide the music. The band was made up of a box-bass, trumpet, mandolin and mouth organ. It was fun to watch the adults dance, especially when Isaac danced with their mother, a rare sight for the children. Albertine looked beautiful and smelled sweet, after daubing essence (perfume) behind her ears and on her wrists, all dolled up in her best satin dress and high-heeled shoes. Isaac as always cut a dashing figure, dressed in a crisply starched, cotton shirt, west-kit and dress pants. He always stood out, his height was unmistakable!

Villagers not only saw the shop as a place to purchase goods. It also served as a meeting place where they gossiped with one another. Isaac did not encourage loitering, but he seemed to accommodate a certain amount of lingering. He became a sounding board for some of the villagers, acquiring private information about the needs and concerns of many. He was a good listener and, being privy to information, was aware of how difficult it was for families to stay connected when members moved away from the village. Isaac thought that the best way to make communication possible was to offer postal services at the shop. There was sufficient space to store and distribute mail and sell stamps. Isaac submitted proposals to provide postal services at his shop to the Warden's Office. The proposals were well received, and he got approval to use the shop as a venue for these services.

Villagers and some from nearby areas were very happy for this added convenience, and made regular visits to send, receive, enquire about mail and or just to purchase stamps. Sometimes villagers who came to the shop to retrieve mail received money in their letters and made purchases before returning home. Hosting these services benefited both the villagers and Isaac. From the time of first approval, there has been uninterrupted access to postal services for villagers and others at Arthur's shop where, today, the shop is a designated TTPost location.[92]

Isaac was now a full-fledged government contractor; he owned his dry goods shop, and a small coconut estate in the area. Workers were paid in cash; there were no banks, checks or ATM's as we have now; any bank that existed was in the capital, Port-of-Spain, and was used by big businessmen only.

Some villagers who worked at other estates in the area travelled to Sangre Grande to collect their wages and chose to purchase their goods at groceries in Sangre Grande. Though convenient for them, the fact that they did, nevertheless, appeared to Isaac as showing a lack of loyalty to him and his shop. He was located nearer to their homes in Rampanalgas, in addition to

---

92 TTPost, Trinidad and Tobago Postal Corporation Limited, is the entity responsible for postal services in Trinidad and Tobago.

which he provided groceries on credit to some of these patrons when they did not have cash.

The workers who purchased groceries in Sangre Grande did not buy kerosene there for fear of spilling it during the trip back to Rampanalgas. Usually a day or two after payday, they would show up at Isaac's shop to purchase kerosene for their lamps. There were occasions when villagers showed up at the shop to obtain groceries on credit, not only during business hours, but sometimes long after the shop was closed for the day. On one occasion, a villager who frequently purchased groceries in Sangre Grande showed up at Isaac's shop for credit. Isaac's response to him was, "Why don't you go back to the *Chineeman* shop in Grande and ask him for credit?"

There were a few villagers who thought that Isaac was mean-spirited. One disgruntled villager was reported to have said, "I wish there was a *Chinee* shop in Rampanalgas, so we don't have to buy at Arthur's." Most of the villagers patronised Isaac's shop and were glad for its convenient location near their homes.

Above:

Kerosene Lamp. Kerosene, a by-product of the petroleum industry was revolutionary. An energy-source, it quickened the march into modern times, bringing a better standard of living for all. Home and street lighting was made possible on a very wide scale, when it was introduced to Port-or-Spain and outlying villages. (Paria Archives)

Above:
1970s Arthur's Grocery & Bar, (Residence in background)

Right:
Arthur Street,
Cumana Village

SAMUEL

Isaac's Son

S amuel, Isaac's first son in his marriage, was born shortly after his parents arrived in Redhead, Cumana Village. As far back as he remembered his days began with chores. Initially they were simple household duties which increased more and more as he got older. One of his primary responsibilities was fetching water from the river which was about half a mile away from their home.

He got up very early in the morning to collect water and fill barrels for the home and the shop, a chore which had to be completed before he left for school. While carrying the large water buckets on his head, he tried to avoid spills as much as possible so as not to have to make additional trips for refills, or he would be late for school. Replenishing the water that was used during the day was a task which had to be completed before sunset. On Saturday, he cut two big bundles of grass to feed the donkeys and mule during the weekend.

At the age of seven, Samuel was sent to the Salybia Government School, Matura. He and his older sister Jane, who was already enrolled there, walked to and from school, about six miles either way from the family home. Samuel believed that Jane had a pair of shoes because she was a girl, but he had none. He learned to move very quickly, practically skimming over patches of road before molten pitch or stones along the gravel path could heat up in the blazing hot, tropical sun. To escape being severely burnt, he sometimes walked on wayside tufts of grass.

By the time Jane completed her schooling, Septie, their younger brother, was ready to attend elementary school. Isaac decided to send both boys, Samuel and Septie, to the Roman Catholic School at Cumana Village. The new school was just about the same distance away as the old one but in the opposite direction. It did not make one bit of difference to the plight of Samuel's feet. The road to Cumana was also pitch and gravel, and he still had no shoes. His bare feet continued to suffer from the sting and bite of the pernicious pavings. Samuel thought his father to be inconsiderate as he did not seem to care; his son walked twelve miles to and from school on bare feet, constantly stubbing and injuring his toes on the stony paths.

Then there was the rainy season from June to November. There was no place to shelter from the rain, except under the trees because houses were recessed from the road. Of course this was useless in a torrential shower. Often Samuel and the other children returned home in soaked clothing and spent the remainder of the day at home. If not, when they arrived at school, wet and uncomfortable, the teacher allowed them to sit in the sun where the feeling of discomfort gradually dissipated as the sun dried their clothing. Despite these discomforts, they were glad to be able to go to school.

Friday, Saturday and sometimes Sunday evenings was an especially happy time for village children when they gathered outdoors to play games. Boys and girls often played together, except when boys pitched marbles or girls played hopscotch.

Everyone ate boiled, roasted or parched corn, a delicious, crunchy treat. Children were happy to shell the dried corn from which the grains were thrown into a big iron pot set up over a stone fire to parch them. Occasionally the pot was stirred to prevent the grains from burning, as some actually popped, making popcorn! Once the grains looked puffy, a mixture of salted water was poured over them and the grains left to dry. This was the equivalent of salted peanuts in the children's world.

Sometimes the children played a game called, *Ship Sail*, with the precious parched or roasted corn grains. While concealing a certain number of grains in the closed fist, the player would recite, *"Ship, sail, sail fast, how many men are on board?"* Everyone guessed. The person who guessed the correct number won the player's hand. Those who guessed an incorrect number had to hand over the number of grains they called to the player! There was always the possibility of losing all of one's treasured grains of corn. This game seemed to be a thinly veiled ruse to get more than one's share, or ironically to lose it.

There's A Brown Girl in the Ring was an all-time favourite. Boys and girls formed a circle and clapped while singing:

> *"There's a brown girl in the ring, tra, la, la la, la...*
> *Girl, show me your motion, tra, la, la,la,la..."*

The person in the centre of the ring danced during the first verse. On the second verse, starting with *"Show me your motion,"* that person showed their moves! On the third verse, the person chose a partner with whom to skip around inside the ring. At the end of the song, the chosen partner became the next *"Brown Girl in the Ring"*. Everyone was given a turn to show their moves.

Sometimes the game was, *Drop Peter Drop* when everyone stood in a circle and sang:

> *"I lost my glove one Saturday night and found it Sunday*
> *morning! Drop Peter!*
> *Drop boy! Peter wouldn't drop boy! Drop Drop! Drop!"*

At the last *"Drop!"* a twig was dropped behind someone in the circle. That person picked up the twig, and ran to catch up with the one who dropped it. The song and activity were repeated until each person had a turn to run around the circle and drop the twig.

Skip or Jump-rope was popular, with many different variations and styles of jumping. The players sang:

> *"Mother in the kitchen, Cooking her chicken, Remember to*
> *add salt, vinegar, mustard, Pepper! Pepper! Pepper!"*

Some children missed the first lines and only knew Pepper! Pepper! Pepper! The repetition of these words energised the persons turning the rope to turn faster, which made the skipper jump faster and higher.

Everyone, adults and children, looked forward to moonlight nights. Silly as it sounds, trapping candle-flies in a glass bottle and pretending it to be a lamp was really entertaining to children back then. But they made sure to avoid any larger than usual candle fly, convinced that it might be a *Soucouyant*![93] This was especially so, after hearing the stories told by the adults who told tales rooted in folklore and legends of the islands. Stories of *Papa Bois*,[94] the old man of the forest who protected the animals from hunters; *Soucouyant*, an old lady of the vampire family who would suck your blood while you slept; *La Diablesse*,[95] the spirit of the wronged woman whose alluring dress concealed one cloven hoof; and *Duenne*,[96] the baby who died without the benefit of baptism. These and a host of other frightful creatures who lived amongst the villagers, unseen.

Of course, there were some children who did not know that the stories were legends and folklore and believed that these creatures really existed. At times stories began with the words, *"Once upon a time...,"* an indication that it was just another Anansi[97] story, a concocted story where the characters were not real people. This was a relief because sometimes the *"Once upon a time"* was not mentioned, and the scary stories persisted. This was serious business![98]

---

93   "It was said long ago that certain French families brought the vampire tradition to Trinidad. These European vampires intermingled with their enslaved African counterparts, and out of this the soucouyant emerged... A soucouyant does not always suck you. She can pinch you too or cuff you" (Besson, "Folklore & Legends of Trinidad and Tobago", 2008, p. 11). See Appendix V (b)

94   "Papa Bois, he is the old man of the forest and is known by many names, including "Maitre Bois" (master of the woods) and "Daddy Bouchon" (Hairy Man). Papa Bois appears in many different forms" (Besson, ibid, p. 11).

95   "As the 'devil woman,' the La Diablesse possesses one cloven hoof, her other foot is elegantly shod. In Trinidad, La Diablesse is the spirit of a woman wronged, and as such she awaits the male predator to take vengeance for transgressions against women" (Besson, ibid, p. 37).

96   Duenne. A baby that died before baptism, returned as "a fat little baby with feet turned backwards and a wide brimmed old-time straw hat on its head." The baby would make a crying sound for attention, which one ignored to avoid dire consequences (Besson, ibid, p. 54).

97   Anansi, a master storyteller, is a character in Caribbean folklore, a cunning trickster generally depicted as a spider with a human head. He is a part of the African Oral Tradition, brought to the Caribbean by way of the Atlantic Slave Trade.

98   Appendix V (c) (ii)

Samuel recalled his father as a stern man who did not tolerate disobedience and firmly believed that to spare the rod was to spoil the child. Isaac was a man of action and very little talk. His instructions were precise and emphatic when he gave assignments. He expected all tasks to be completed to his satisfaction and within a specific time frame. There were those which had to be done before going to school in the morning, and others after school but before sunset in the evening. Yet, from time to time, Samuel ran afoul of his father and suffered the consequences.

When he was about nine or ten years old one of his chores was collecting firewood for the oven. One Saturday morning when he went to the forest, he ran into some schoolmates who were also sent to collect firewood. They decided to play a quick game of marbles. After locating a good spot, the mates cleared away some bushes and prepared the area for play. They became so engrossed in the game that they lost track of time.

Samuel only became aware that hours had passed when he felt hungry. He had not gathered any firewood and his mother would be waiting to cook the family lunch. Knowing what lay in store for him, he decided to trick his way out of the situation. He hurriedly gathered a few twigs, bundled them as he ran home and lay them down quietly, hoping not to be noticed. He entered the kitchen and asked his mother for lunch. Eyeing the small bundle of twigs he had laid down, she questioned, "Where have you been all morning? Pappy has your lunch."

He pretended not to know why his father had his lunch and asked, "Pappy, can I please have my lunch?" With his eyes fixed on the small bundle of twigs, Pappy replied, "No! I want you to account for your long absence." Turning towards Samuel he continued, "You mean to say that since morning when you left here, this is all the firewood you collected? Now let me see how long it will take you to collect a proper bundle. When you do, your lunch will be in your hands."

Even though his mother was not pleased with him, she knew that Samuel had not eaten any breakfast and that he was hungry. As he went past the kitchen, she handed him a piece of bread and whispered, "This should keep you going for now."

Samuel left home disappointed and headed to the forest. This time he was alone, angry and frustrated. He concentrated his efforts on collecting a substantial bundle of good quality firewood which he felt confident would please his Father. As soon as he got home, he went straight to him and showed him the bundle he had collected. Nodding his satisfaction, Isaac turned to his wife and said, "You see? You have to starve them sometimes for them to complete their chores."

Sometimes his punishment was harsher. One night Samuel and Septie ran away from home to attend a wake. They had always been curious about wakes but had never been allowed to attend one. That night, they decided to bypass asking for their father's permission to attend. Instead, they let their sisters in on their plans to steal out. When they felt sure that both parents were asleep, they climbed out the window. Samuel stuck a wood chip between the window-sill and frame, so that the window appeared to be closed. He planned to remove the chip to reopen it on their return.

They ran through the bushes to the dead-house which was lit by flambeaux attached to poles on the outside, and candle-light which flickered on the inside. It was easy to see into the house because the curtains had been removed. A few women appeared to be engaged in some type of activity, but they were unable to tell what. They decided to lay low and stay outside so that they would not be seen and reported to their father. From where they stood, they observed a big iron pot from which clouds of steam and a mouth-watering smell wafted. Two older men played cards next to a shed where another two were engaged in sawing and hammering. They later found out that the men were building the coffin, while the women inside the house were measuring and sewing the shroud.

As if on cue, two men with drums began a soft drumming which gradually grew louder. A few people began dancing while two instigators produced a length of bamboo which instantly prompted Limbo dancing. Unable to resist the pulsating music and mesmerizing dancers, the boys forgot their resolve to lay low and, as if propelled by invisible hands, were drawn to the middle of the dance where after stumbling into the rhythm, they learnt a few Bongo steps. They became so absorbed with dancing that they did not hear or reply when someone asked, "Does your Father know that you are out here?" It was way past midnight and into the wee hours of the morning when they made their way back home. As they approached the yard, the dogs began to bark, their barking became a whimper when they recognised Samuel and Septie who had no idea that the whimper was a sign of what was to come.

Samuel went to the window where he had placed the wood chip. It was gone and the window was tightly shut! He tried to prise the window open, but it was locked from the inside. He next went to his sisters' window to ask for help, when he was told that Isaac had checked their beds and bolted the window shut when he realised that they were not in their room. The girls had been warned by Isaac that if anyone opened the windows to let their brothers in, they would be punished too!

Determined to get into the house without his Father knowing, Samuel went to the kitchen at the back of the house and found a knife. He pushed it into a crevice to rattle the latch, until the window eventually opened. Relieved, they climbed into the room, only to hear Pappy clearing his throat as they landed. Surprised, and not knowing what to do, they lay down pretending to be asleep, snoring and all! Pappy questioned them about where they went and immediately disciplined them when they were through with their story.

In Rampanalgas Village where everyone knew the family, it was impossible to hide. The following morning a villager who came to the shop said, "Mr. Isaac! We saw your sons at the wake last night!" Isaac's response was, "Yes... and they paid the price!"

Assignments

"Everything had to be done to his satisfaction."

Samuel believed his father thought him capable, and expected him to act as such, promptly and efficiently. As he grew older, he seemed to understand that his father's intentions towards him were to have him be responsible, reliable, and a successful man who would make his father proud. At the time when he played marbles instead of collecting firewood, his father taught him a lesson of work followed by reward: he gave him his lunch. On another occasion when he and his brother Septie ran away to attend a wake, his father was unsparing of the rod and chastised them both, and was particularly hard on him as the older brother who should have known better. However, now that Samuel was older, his father was getting on his nerves.

Samuel did not enjoy doing all these chores. He believed that his father knew that he was resentful, even as he insisted that the chores had to be completed satisfactorily. He believed that he had no choice, and often thought of being away from home, where he could be independent and not have to follow his father's rules. He greatly resented the disciplinarian behaviour which in retrospect he thought was his father's way of preparing him to face life.

Just after turning fifteen, Samuel completed primary school. He was now spending most of his time hanging around the house. His mother was quite happy for his company, but he was restless. He had become disenchanted with life in the village. There had been no mention of his going on to secondary school because, perhaps, his father was not willing or able to meet the cost of sending him to school in Sangre Grande or even further away to Port-of-Spain.

One day, Isaac asked him, "Young man, what do you plan to do with yourself now that you are finished with school?" Samuel replied that he was interested in becoming a mechanic. Isaac pointed out that there was no real opportunity to train as a mechanic in the area. But, he was encouraging. He explained to Samuel that there would be more opportunities for that type of work around San Fernando, the island's industrial capital. He promised to talk to Clifford, his wife's brother who lived in Marabella which was not far from San Fernando, to see what could be done. Soon after, Samuel was on his way to his uncle's house.

The Mechanic

A person engaged in repairing vehicle engines

It was 1943 and Samuel was almost 17 years old. He was tall for his age, almost as tall as his father. He was treated as an adult by strangers because of his height. Now on his way to Marabella, he walked through Cunapo to await the train to Port-of-Spain. Samuel had been here before with his father when they attended the Sangre Grande Magistrate's Court[99]. Then and now he was dumbstruck by the amount of people going to and fro within the area. Here there were more people in one place than he had ever seen: men riding bicycles, donkey carts, women with baskets, all seemed to be caught up in a whirl of activity. He wondered how they knew which way to go without bumping into each other. He walked in his new shoes on the asphalt-paved roads, experiencing a slight bounce partly due to the softness of the sun-hot asphalt.

The courthouse was a cream coloured, wooden, two-story building, standing next to the police station and a small jailhouse. The police station opened onto the traffic flow that became the Roundabout. He could not help noticing the very tall *poui* tree whose branches extended above the police station, and the many bird nests hanging from its branches. The unexpected sight presented a pause amidst all the bustle.

Changing trains when he arrived at Port-of-Spain, allowed Samuel a chance to get a brief peek at the city. He could glimpse sheets of dark seas where huge ships docked on the wharf, across from the majestically tree-lined promenade which was Marine Square. This was unlike anywhere he had ever seen before. He thought of returning to the city as soon as he could to do some sightseeing.

At first the train ride to Marabella seemed tedious, when the train stopped for passengers to disembark and waited for others to board. After a few stops, the train picked up speed, whooshing past tall green cane fields; plains dotted by lagoons of still water appearing mirror-like where they reflected the overhead sun and small boxy houses held up by tall narrow pillars—out of place *moko jumbies* where they dotted the landscape.

Marabella was a stone's throw away from San Fernando.

Uncle Clifford was a blacksmith who worked at the nearby Pointe-à-Pierre oil field. He lived with his family, a wife and daughter. Later Samuel found out that his uncle belonged to The Faith Healing School of Christianity Church[100] where he was a lay reader. This was the same denomination to which Isaac belonged. Samuel sometimes attended services with his uncle, he even befriended some of the younger members, but he was not quite ready for this new lifestyle. He missed the interaction with his siblings and visited them whenever he could.

---

99   Appendix II (c) (i)

100   The Faith Healing School of Christianity Church was affiliated to Pentecostal churches in Trinidad.

Back at Rampanalgas, there were no churches when Samuel grew up. The nearest ones were in Cumana and Matura. Even though his father belonged to a faith, he never insisted on the children attending services. Samuel's view was that his father's businesslike attitude more than made up for the religiosity associated with churchgoing. Later in life, he attended church with his wife, but religion was not a major feature in his life as a young man.

Samuel admired his uncle whom he said invariably had a good attitude. He was always dressed in his robe and slippers around the house, had breakfast at a well set table, and always said grace before meals. After nearly eight months of living at Uncle Clifford, Samuel asked another aunt who lived in San Fernando, if he could stay at her home. Wondering what his father and uncle would think of this request, he was pleasantly surprised when they agreed to the idea.

Soon after moving to his aunt's home at San Fernando, she secured a job for him as an apprentice mechanic with the Lazzari Garage & Trucking Company. Life at his Auntie was good, even though she and her husband were always sparring; she seemed determined to convert her husband to her denomination while he was just as determined not to be converted. He was adamant in his refusal to join her church and was not about to give up his congregation in Jesus' Almighty Name! Samuel found these moments when he overheard their interactions amusing. His aunt was doing well at her job until her husband lost his eyesight, and she was forced to give up her job, to devote more time to her husband.

Samuel continued to live at his Aunt's home, and was happy for the opportunity to work with mechanics. The pay at Lazzari was good, five dollars every Friday. He gave his aunt money for board and lodging, and kept the change for movies which were silent and westerns. He usually sat in the pit, the least expensive and rowdiest part of the hall where the loud comments of some patrons was a show all by itself!

After about ten months on the job, Samuel was laid off. He was unable to find a replacement job, so he said goodbye to his aunt and headed for Port-of-Spain where one of his older sisters Eldica lived at 4A Harper Lane, Belmont. Eldica and her husband welcomed him into their home, inviting him to stay as long as he wished.

Samuel was fortunate to get a job as an apprentice at Sam's Garage where the pay was even better than at Lazzari. Eleven dollars a week, a six dollar increase over his previous salary! After working for about five months, he was laid off because of a shortage of car parts due to the war.

The Second World War was happening and there was a shortage of imported car parts that were either delayed in transit or no longer available due to war prioritising. Samuel was no longer employed, and finding a job proved impossible. He had no choice but to return to Rampanalgas, and Isaac's assignments.

Samuel believed that even though his efforts at becoming a mechanic did not turn out quite as he expected, they were well worth the effort. During the time he spent between San Fernando and Port-of Spain as an apprentice, just about two and a half years, he gathered knowledge and skills about engines and motor transport which he was able to use later. Best of all, he had experienced a taste of working for himself, living away from his father, and making his own money. He had also connected with relatives and made new friends.

"Suzie and Sambo"[101]

The Coconut grating machine "Suzie" devised by Isaac, and the pot used for boiling the coconut milk which was referred to as "Sambo."

When Samuel returned home from his stint as a mechanic his father was well established in his role as a government contractor responsible for the development of local roads, with the ability to hire whom he chose. In addition, he owned a coconut estate where he provided employment for some of the villagers. Samuel approached his father and asked him for a job, to which his father responded, "I cannot offer you a permanent position, but I can help you with a part-time job working with me." The 'part-time job working with me' turned out to be whatever needed to be done at a moment's notice or no notice at all.

Samuel was given a variety of assignments which appeared to have no rhyme or reason. Old resentments resurfaced, but he also knew that if he dared voice his displeasure he would lose his 'part-time job'. Samuel worked in this situation for five long years. The tasks he was assigned included grating the nuts for making coconut oil. This was a different home-grown venture Isaac had going, separate from producing copra. The products of both ventures ended up at the Coconut Growers Association.[102]

Grating coconuts was a very demanding task, which had to be done soon after the nuts were removed from the shells because the kernels would become rancid and unsuitable for making oil, resulting in a financial loss to Isaac. Usually there was a large number of nuts to grate. It was a very time-consuming process, not to mention the pain of grating one's own fingers on the sharp grater.

The ingenious Isaac constructed a machine they called "Suzie" to grate the nuts. It was fast, produced more meal, and eliminated the discomfort of grating by hand. It saved a lot of time and effort. It was this display of intelligence and creativity that Samuel so often saw in Isaac that caused him to admire his father, in spite of the bitterness he felt. His resentment was made deeper by the fact that Isaac treated him like a hired hand and not as a son. Once again, he began to think of getting away.

---

101 Appendix III (d)

102 In 1937 Estate owners from across the islands came together to form the Coconut Growers Association. A year later, they commissioned a central mill in Laventille where all copra could be brought and processed. The location has never changed. https://cgacaribbean.com

One day, Isaac gave him the assignment to weed the pea garden he had planted close to the road. Even though the sun was very hot, he was expected to weed the garden immediately. After he gave Samuel the assignment, Isaac left home to go hunting. As soon as his father was gone, Samuel decided to make his move and leave home. He went to his mother and told her his decision. She tried to talk him out of it , but his mind was made up. His mother was not angry with him, and he believed she understood how he felt; she gave him some cash when he said his goodbyes and departed.

Earlier in the day, Samuel had noticed a Lazzari truck delivering pitch in the area. After the workers completed their delivery, he asked for a ride with them to Port-of-Spain. When he was dropped off in the city, Samuel headed right back to his sister Eldica to ask her for lodging. She was happy as always to see him and welcomed him back to her home.

Samuel kept in contact with his mother while he tried to get a job at a garage, but his attempts were fruitless. While job hunting, he met his friend, Francois, who lived at Harp Place and worked at Angostura.[103] Francois helped him to get a job there. The pay was seven dollars and twenty cents weekly. From this pay packet he saved, paid for meals, and was still able to dress fashionably like his friends. Even though he missed his family, Samuel had the camaraderie of friends who drank rum after lunch every day. Unfortunately, he did not keep a check on the amount of rum he consumed, in addition to which he did not eat nutritious meals. A bad combination he soon found out, when he began to feel the effects of over-indulgence in too much rum and too little food. Samuel paid dearly for this mistake. Meanwhile, he was doing well, and life was good.

At Christmas time, Samuel and his friends from the country went home for the holidays. By this time, there was a bus stop in front of Arthur's shop; it had become a known landmark for people in the area. The stop was both a good and a bad marker, since everyone getting on or off the bus could be seen from the shop. When Samuel alighted from the bus and began walking up the incline to his parents' home, he heard his father shouting from the shop. "Hello, young man! Where do you think you are going? Not up here! Not up here!" Samuel could tell from the tone of his father's voice that he was not pleased to see him. All he could do was wave to his mother and sisters and return to the bus. He ended up staying at a friend's house. During Boxing Day holiday, the day after Christmas, after Isaac left the house, Samuel was alerted that his father had gone out; he took the opportunity to visit his mother and siblings, and deliver the Christmas presents he had brought them.

Shortly after Samuel returned to Port-of-Spain, he fell ill. Once again he was forced to return to his parents' home, this time to recuperate. Isaac did not have anything to say, but Samuel believed he felt sad about his

---

103   The House of Angostura, famous for its bitters, also makes rum. It is located in Laventille, Port-of-Spain, Trinidad and Tobago.

son's state. It took a few months for Samuel to finally pull himself together, and even then he decided to spend some more time at home since he was not completely mended. He gave up his apartment in the city, and had his clothing brought to him.

Men who considered themselves to be at the cutting edge of fashion at the time, 'town man' imitated the zoot suit, patterned after those worn by Cab Calloway,[104] the famed black American singer who dubbed the zoot suit, "the ultimate in clothes." The jacket was long, and fell to mid-thigh. The knee area of the pants was wide, tapering down to the ankle. This was accessorised by a long gold fob chain, attached at the waist, which dropped at the front of the pants. An Adams hat made of straw or felt was worn along with Cuban heeled shoes which completed the outfit.

Isaac did not approve of the style, and warned Samuel, "Do not wear those fancy pants in my house because if you do I will cut them up." His mother, on the other hand, loved how he looked in his outfits which he wore well because of his tall slender build. Albertine was very aware of Isaac's rules for the home and encouraged Samuel to make adjustments to compromise with his father's wishes. He decided not to wear the pants and chose to wear clothing that would meet his father's approval: workman's clothing, blue-dock (denim) or khaki pants with a white terylene shirt.

This situation reminded him of his father's admonition when the boys were younger, and he warned them that they were not allowed to whistle under his roof. What a man!

Samuel enjoyed living in the country, but he kept thinking of his next job. He wanted to be a mechanic but his attempts as an apprentice had been short-lived due to layoffs and garage closures during the war. It was 1953, and he decided to try another option. He applied for a temporary position with the Telephone Company (Telco), figuring that once he got a foot in the door, it would be easier to get a permanent position. Samuel told his Father of his plans while he continued to work with him. Soon after he applied, the telephone company recruited him as a "leave relief".

Samuel returned to Port of Spain to work and now lived in the city. His workplace was on Frederick Street at the company's main office. Here he often ran into people he knew, some from back home in the country, including one relative whom he saw quite often, his cousin Sydney Arthur. When Sydney saw him coming he would say, "Ah smellin ah Arthur! Give me ah 'grease hand', nuh boy." Samuel usually gave him some change, with which he would always buy a 'petit quart.' One day Samuel asked him, "Why don't you buy a bigger bottle? He responded, "I don't need to attract flies."

Samuel was given a supervisory position in record time. His job now entailed traveling to different parts of the city to do assessments and repairs. One day he was asked to go to the St. Ann's Mental Hospital to do a job.

---

104   Appendix X (a). Cabell "Cab" Calloway III, (December 25, 1907–November 18, 1994,) was an American jazz singer, dancer and bandleader who famously performed at Harlem's Cotton Club in New York.

He had never been there before, but he knew that his oldest brother Jacob, Isaac's first son, was institutionalised there.

Above:

This is what Samuel's journey to and from school may have looked like.
(Paria Archives, Fern Mackenzie Collection)

Above:

Boys focused on the game. Pitching marbles was serious business. Samuel often kept his marbles on him so he would never miss a chance to play a quick game.
(Paria Archives)

Above:

The train on its way to San Fernando.
(Paria Archives)

Left:

Passenger cars in Port-of-Spain train station. (Paria Archives)

Right:
Sugar cane as far as the eye can see. San Fernando. (Paria Archives)

Above:
Globe Cinema in Port-of-Spain, with the famous Green Corner in the foreground and an officer crossing the intersection of St. Vincent and Park Street. (Paria Archives, Fern Mackenzie Collection)

Above:

Angostura workers on the factory floor, bottling bitters. (Paria Archives)

Above:

 An example of what a bitters bottle would have looked like at the time.

(Paria Archives)

Left:

Norfolk Street, Belmont. What Belmont looked like.

(Paria Archives, Fern Mackenzie Collection)

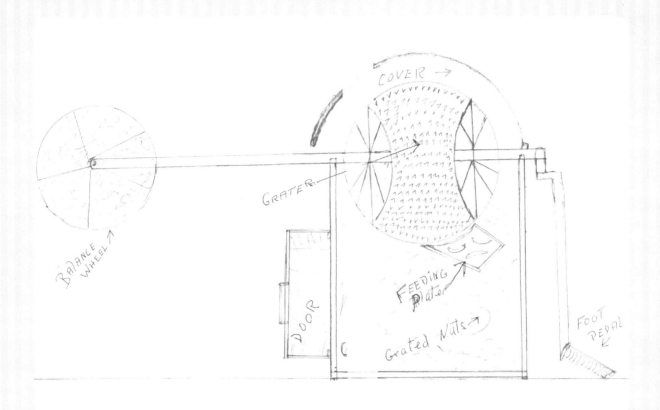

COVER →

GRATER

BALANCE WHEEL ↑

DOOR

FEEDING Plate

Grated Nuts →

FOOT PEDAL ↓

Above:
"Suzie and Sambo"
A representation of Isaac's coconut grating machine and Photo of machine modeled after Isaac's in use at Samuel's home in Blanchisseuse.

Above:

Telephone poles line the side walk, as do taxi-cars, while a tram goes by on Frederick Street, Port-of-Spain.

Country life is sweet but the possibility of being a mechanic was always on Samuel's mind.
(Paria Publishing, Fern Mackenzie Collection)

Above:
Samuel Arthur - 1950s

Above:
Samuel Arthur - 2017

Left:
Cab Calloway in
zoot suit.

Above:
Samuel clearly had a
good sense of fashion.

JACOB'S LADDER

The bridge between heaven and earth.

I t was while he worked at the Telephone Company that Samuel reunited with his brother, Jacob. Samuel recalled that in the late 1930s when he was still a teenager, a stranger had come to the house. He was a tall, light-skinned man, with "interesting features and a large afro". He must have walked a long distance because he appeared very tired. Isaac casually said to the children who were gaping at the stranger, "This young man is your brother, Jacob".

Isaac gave Jacob a room at the back of the house. In return Jacob was expected to assist with work on the property but he had other plans. Jacob befriended the young men in the neighbourhood and took to gambling behind his father's house. Neighbours reported this activity to Isaac who immediately put an end to it and dispatched him to Cumana to handle his coconut interests there.

However, Isaac's hope that Jacob would become industrious and self-sufficient were soon dashed. The house on the property in Cumana was occupied by one of Isaac's sisters and other relatives. Jacob took charge of things in his own way. He appointed himself overseer and forbade his relatives from harvesting the coconuts. He was at constant loggerheads with his relatives, and when seized by fits of rage because his orders were not obeyed, he would proceed to break up household items. Of course, Isaac's sister reported this behaviour to her brother.

Isaac confronted Jacob and gave him an ultimatum. Jacob's response was a demand for "my piece of land". He let it be known that he should be able to do whatever he wished with the land he was claiming as his, including "not work on my land". It appeared that he wished to goad Isaac into giving him the land by issuing his own ultimatum: either give him the land or remove his name from the deed. Isaac was not a man to be trifled with. He immediately journeyed to Port-of-Spain and had Mr. Annisette, his lawyer, draw up papers to remove Jacob's claim on the property.

Jacob left Cumana Village and returned to the capital where he apparently enlisted in the armed services. He came back to Cumana about six years later. This time he brought with him three women of obvious ill-repute! They were welcomed by some of the local men, but the villagers were not about to tolerate the disreputable lifestyle and quickly drove them out. Then came the report that Jacob was "reading bad books", a euphemism for dabbling in the occult. At the same time, curiously, he was also reported to be cohabiting with "a very Christian young lady whom he had inveigled to live with him in the bushes and who had become pregnant." When Isaac received these reports, he again confronted Jacob who responded in typical fashion and destroyed household items. Isaac had had enough; he reported Jacob to the police and had him arrested and charged.

Villagers flocked to the weekly Cumana Magistrates Court hearing which Isaac did not attend. Upon hearing another case called before his, Jacob jumped up and said, "Out of turn," without his lawyer entering a plea. When his turn came, he pled guilty. The outcome was, "Immediate assessment at the St. Ann's Mental Hospital, in the Black Maria."[105] *En route* the Black Maria stopped at the family shop where Jacob was spotted at the back of the vehicle. That was the last anyone saw of him, until...

It was 1955 and Samuel was now a supervisor for the Telephone Company. He was given an assignment at the aforementioned St. Ann's Hospital and took the opportunity to see his brother. He disclosed some of his brother's story to colleagues who felt that Jacob was non-threatening and could not understand why he was *"in the madhouse"*. Samuel developed a relationship with Jacob and visited him as often as he could. In the spirit of reciprocity, Jacob gifted him a loaf of bread on one occasion, (Like his father Isaac, and his grandfather, Joseph Arthur, it appears that Jacob was an excellent baker) and informed him that he was good at making all kinds of sweet treats and worked at the hospital's bakery.

During these visits Jacob questioned Samuel about his life. He asked whether Samuel was married and whether he lived alone. Samuel wasn't sure why Jacob asked these questions. He had been keeping Isaac abreast of his visits to Jacob, and Isaac didn't seem to care one way or another. However, when Samuel told him that Jacob had asked for a T-shirt, a pair of trousers and sneakers in a specific size, Isaac forbade him to continue the visits. Samuel stayed away for some time, but Jacob intrigued him and he resumed the visits. Then one day, Jacob told him, just like that, "They are going to do a big operation on my head!"

Jacob died during the surgery...

---

105   The transport used to convey convicted persons directly from the Courthouse to the Jail.

Above:
Recent photos taken of St. Ann's "Mental Hospital" Psychiatric Hospital.

Left:
St. Ann's Mental Hospital.
(Paria Archives)

Above:
Ladies walking along telephone lined St. Ann's Road, the northern boundary of the Savannah, looking north
towards the St. Ann's Mental Hospital. The saaman tree on the left is still here to today.
(Paria Archives)

Above:

The St. Ann's Tram arriving at the Port-of-Spain Transfer Station.

(Paria Archives, Fern Mackenzie Collection)

Above:

Tram driver and conductors.

(Paria Archives)

ISAAC'S LEGACY

Isaac's original venture, the dry-goods shop, along with the business enterprises which grew up around it, have been improved and extended.

Isaac worked every day, decreasing his activities on Saturday, and doing only essentials on Sunday. He lived by the adage, *"Early to bed, early to rise,"* going to bed at 7:00 o'clock in the evening and rising at 5:00 o' clock in the morning. His routine started with morning prayers, followed by a walk, sometimes across the street to the beach, where he swam for about an hour, or at times he just followed the path of the river bank. On his return, he had tea[106] and opened the shop.

Breakfast was at 12:00 noon and dinner at 5:00 o' clock. Except for when he travelled on business, there were seldom any variations to this routine.

He went about his life in a purposeful way, focusing his talents on building the tiny hamlet of Rampanalgas. Clever, resourceful and skillful with his hands, he adapted the clay oven for his wife's convenience, as he did with the coconut grating machine he constructed *"Suzie."* This machine was efficient and convenient, lightening the unpleasant task of grating coconuts.

Interactions with the oldest son of his marriage, appear to be harsh when aggregated: bare feet; burdensome chores; absence of educational guidance—the latter leaves one to wonder, at the omission of further education in one as ambitious and worldly as Isaac? He had the resources (money) to send his son to school in the city, or even if the aptitude was lacking, he had contacts, to arrange for formal training in a skilled trade, maybe as a mechanic, in which his son expressed his interest. Even though his achievements were above average, Isaac was a product of his time, caught in the common trap of some parents who thought it a 'Rite of Passage,' to allow their children to experience similar types of hardships like they did while growing up.

Isaac loved making pastries. It is possible that he might have learned this skill from his father although it is not certain how close the relationship between father and son were. Similarly, the proficiency in baking his son Jacob displayed could have been acquired from contact with Isaac although there is no evidence that they ever lived together. One wonders whether this manifestation of skillful hands was some inborn trait passed on through

---

106   Villagers from rural areas often referred to Breakfast as "tea", lunch as "breakfast" and supper as "dinner".

generations. This domestic variance in his habits did not translate into preparation of regular family meals which he left up to his wife. He was particular about what he ate, and did not buy food prepared by strangers, preferring to bring along his wife's coconut bake sandwiches for his meals when travelling to Port-of-Spain on business.

Although Isaac was a stern disciplinarian, he never raised his voice, but made his point emphatically and clearly so that everyone understood what he meant. He was not only insistent that rules be upheld by other persons, but he also applied rules in his own home.

For example, he admonished anyone whistling in his house, by saying, "I am the only man who can whistle in this house, and you boys would have to whistle under your own roof".

Calypso singing was not tolerated in the home, and his children could only sing hymns or school songs. This was not an uncommon demand in homes where parents strove to keep children from being exposed to indecency.

Isaac maintained a relationship with his three adult children who lived in different parts of Port-of-Spain. They were known to the children of his marriage so that Samuel felt comfortable turning up at his sister Eldica's home when he needed a place to stay. Despite his debacle with eldest son Jacob, Isaac offered him a place to live and a chance to settle his life. Isaac spent the final months of his life at the home of his other daughter, Jestina, from where he had convenient access to his physicians. It appears that Isaac also maintained an amicable relationship with his daughter from Sierra Village, Delia, whom Samuel mentioned was always welcome at the family home, and her mother was treated with respect.

Isaac's first venture, *"Arthur's Shop,"* now known as *"Arthurs' Grocery & Bar,"* which he started at Rampanalgas Village in 1927, outlived the man, and continues to thrive on the spot where he started. The shop will have served the community for 100 years in 2027. The shop, along with the business enterprises which grew up around it, have been improved and extended. The parlour, where he sold drinks, pastries and food, continues as Kay's Pot and Jenny's Kitchen, two food service establishments which have been added to the site. A hotel, *D'Arthurs Hotel*, a full service 'Rest Stop' has been erected on the adjoining lot. They are now owned and managed by his daughter Greta, her children and grandchildren, along with various extended family members—a testament to Isaac Arthur's dedication and determination. The venue, where he first received approval to provide postal services is now a TTPost Outlet.

Isaac petitioned the government for amenities needed to develop and expand the village. In his role as a government contractor, he opened job opportunities for villagers, when secondary roads were built in the village, laying the infrastructure for further development of the area. He created work on his small coconut estate, for climbers, gatherers, nut processors and even the women who gathered the pieces of nuts as they fell to the ground, bagging them, for transport and drying. The business produced both copra and coconut oil adding to the Gross Domestic Product and overall exports from the country, through the Coconut Growers Association.

Isaac's influence was both enabling and supportive in several spheres, particularly when he allowed a private school to be housed on his property. When the owner of the only school in the village, a kindergarten level, private school, was unable to carry on, he paid a replacement teacher out of his own pocket. He secured the designation of land for a burial ground in Rampanalgas, so that villagers no longer suffered the inconveniences associated with travel to Cumana to bury their loved ones. He also secured the designation of land for a recreation ground, a venue for young people to play sports and engage in social activities. One cannot help but reiterate the sentiments of descendants and knowledgeable villagers. The recreation ground is currently named after someone who was

Above:

Greta Arthur, Isaac's daughter, resides at the original Arthur's home, where she and her extended family continue to run the family businesses.

said to have had less to do with its inception and recreational usefulness than that of Isaac Arthur.

The introduction of pipe-borne water flowing in the homes of villagers, was Isaac's final wish for Rampanalgas Village. This wish was granted two weeks before he died in 1959.

Above:
Arthur's Grocery and Bar.

Above:
D Arthur's Hotel, Restaurant and Conference Centre.

ALPHEUS

My father Alpheus Scobie was dark chocolate brown in complexion, of medium height and slim build. He was a good-looking gentleman with a serious countenance, quiet reserve and polite demeanour. To some he appeared to be stern and strict, but in time it became apparent that during actual interaction, he had a ready smile which reached his eyes, highlighting his round pleasant face.

Alpheus was born at Lambeau, Tobago, in 1910, and brought to Cumana Village, Trinidad, as a baby. Soon after his arrival, the lamentable circumstances of his mother's committal and confinement occurred. Fortunately, his mother's sister, Rebecca, Aunt Becca, took charge of her baby nephew and from thereon assumed the responsibility for his care. Relatives recalled that Aunt Becca favoured him, and it is quite likely that other relatives were also fond of him given their regular visits to his home.

My father never told us what he knew about his mother. In fact, he didn't talk about his childhood. I could only imagine that the circumstances of his mother's commitment and the separation of the children were considered issues best left in the past. I get the impression that my relatives were people who bravely did what had to be done to get on with the business of life. They were practical people who would see no usefulness in burdening children with adult matters. Besides, Mary's lunacy must have been a source of embarrassment in a village where everyone knew everyone.

Perhaps it was Alpheus' good fortune that he was raised by Aunt Becca whose affection and nurturing served him in good stead; he would become a disciplined, industrious man, and honest. This was not the case of Edward who was seven years older than Alpheus and grew up with his father James. I can only guess that James, initially devastated by his wife's absence, went on with his life: he had a good job, some land on which he reared cattle, and, as Rufus recalled, was fond of the ladies. His son Edward was responsible for cutting grass to feed the cattle. One day, for whatever reason, he cut grass from a neighbour's property. The neighbour reported Edward to the police who arrested and charged Edward with praedial larceny.[107] Edward was sentenced to incarceration at the Youth Training Centre (YTC)[108] where youthful offenders were held. This turned out to be a blessing in disguise for Edward. He learned carpentry at the YTC and went on to become a successful master carpenter.

Alpheus attended the Anglais Anglican School where he was taught the *three Rs*.[109] He left primary school as a teenager with just enough skills to lead a hand-to-mouth existence. Primary level education, available to all, was the end of the road in terms of education for most young people at the time. There was not much to look forward to in the village after primary school, except some form of manual labour. Choices were limited in this rural community to agricultural pursuits like planting provisions, working on a cocoa or coconut estate, or possibly 'days work' on the Toco Main Road. Those who could manage, might go on to learn a trade, and those who had both the aptitude and finances went on to further their education, some emerging as recognised professionals. But these were fairly rare.[110]

In 1926, Alpheus was sixteen years old when his Uncle Isaac arrived at Redhead, Cumana Village. It seems that though he had not been offered an opportunity to acquire a trade, he was fortunate to get a job helping out at his Uncle Isaac's newly opened dry-goods shop. I imagine Alpheus must have been relieved and thrilled to be associated with his uncle. Here was the ideal father-figure, a handsome man of means who wielded authority. However, just as he was becoming used to the idea of being around him, his Uncle Isaac passed the shop to his sister Annie, and relocated to Sierra Village, a much smaller community in the region. Isaac's departure may have dampened young Alpheus' spirits because even though Aunt Annie was much loved and he continued to work with her, the unexpected change in circumstances did not do much to engender his confidence in a future for himself in Cumana.

I believe that while working at his Aunt's shop, Alpheus had lots of time to ponder his situation, and he had no intention of becoming trapped like his brother Edward. He knew that he did not have much to look forward to in Cumana Village. It was not just the bleakness of the future that caused him anxiety. He had heard that some villagers, including young men whom he knew had begun to indulge in occult practises, reading 'bad books',[111] and

---

107 "Praedial Larceny," a term peculiar to the Caribbean, is the theft of agricultural produce. The Praedial Larceny Prevention Act is codified in The Laws of Trinidad and Tobago.

108 The Youth Training Centre (YTC), was a reform school patterned after those set up in Britain in 1854 and replicated in the colonies. Youthful offenders were sent here as an alternative to adult prison.

109 Appendix IX (b)

110 Mr. Charles Wheeler (Peter Cordner's son-in-law), became the headmaster of the Anglais Anglican School.

111 Books dealing with the occult, the supernatural and unexplained.

assuming the forms of *Legahoo*[112] and *La Diablesse*[113] for diabolical purposes. These stories were pervasive, and some relatives were even believed to practice the behaviours.

Salvation came to Alpheus. The Seventh Day Adventists, a Christian denomination founded in the United States in the 1860s, had reached Trinidad. The Adventists were set apart from other denominations in their strict adherence to keeping the Sabbath on the seventh day of the week, in accordance with the fourth commandment. Supplemental teachings by one of the prophets Ellen G. White[114] offered guidance in the more practical aspects of a healthy lifestyle like vegetarianism which Alpheus later embraced.

The evangelical strategy of the Adventists was the *crusade*, a series of outdoor meetings held in a canvas tent, pitched in a conspicuous location to attract attention. Here the preacher expounded *The Three Angels Message*[115], the foundation of their faith. The meetings were a carefully calibrated effort between visiting members; interested persons recruited from the area; and preferably, a foreign evangelist chosen for his soul-stirring articulation of *The Message*. The sermons, preceded by a lusty song service, set one up for the message which unfailingly ended in 'a call,' a well crafted scene which brought on waves of guilt liberally sprinkled with anxiety as to the immediate fate of one's soul.

The Adventists offered Alpheus far more than the salvation of his soul. A young convert such as himself had the opportunity to attend the Caribbean Training College,[116] now known as the University of The Southern Caribbean, which was founded, owned and operated by Seventh-Day-Adventists. The only requirements for entrance to the college were membership in the faith, a willing and industrious spirit, and a simple work tool such as a cutlass or a hoe[117].

---

112   Legahoo: a mythical shape-shifting creature which can transform into various animals, including donkeys, pigs, dogs, goats, animals that appear normal by day, but take on the form of a man with no head who roams by night.

113   La Diablesse: typically a vengeful being, a woman who appears gorgeous from far away, wearing a big, wide brimmed hat that covers her face, and a long dress that covers her goat hoof. She sometimes walks with one leg on the road, and the other hoofs in the bush to hide it.

114   Ellen G. White - A prophetess and co-founder of the Seventh-Day-Adventist Church, whose many writings were said to be inspired by visions, laid out a guide for daily life.

115   The Three Angels Message from The Book of Revelation as told in The King James Version of The Bible, urging preparation and foretelling the second coming of Christ.

116   Appendix IX (a)

117   I was first told of the *"cutlass or hoe"* entrance requirement to attend CTC by Mrs Cojer Pritchard. This information was reiterated by her cousin, Priscilla Alexander, the daughter of Nathan Alexander, an original recruit to the College. Priscilla explained that the tools were needed to cut and clear the many acres of trees and bush present during construction of the College. Conversations held on January1, 2021 and March 15, 2021 with Mrs Cojer-Pritchard and Priscilla Alexander respectively.

Caribbean Training College and Getting Married

Alpheus moved away from Cumana Village sometime in the 1930s, most likely after the Toco Main Road was opened. This would have been around the same time that other family members of his generation, whose parents had done well during the cocoa boom, were moving out of the Toco Region to pursue further education and training. Monetizing whatever little he got from his father, he packed his grip, and headed to Caribbean Training College (CTC).

This fledgling institution was sheltered under the protective flank of the Northern Range, recessed in the verdant forests of Maracas Valley, St Joseph, a village famous for its picturesque waterfall. The campus was established away from the distractions of city-life, in an atmosphere meant to thoroughly ground its graduates in a lifestyle that would set them apart from the world. Here training focused on life skills and the vocations of Bible Workers, Colporteurs, and Pastors.

My father met my mother while he was a student. They would get married in 1939. Confident that he could call upon his well-to-do Uncle Isaac for financial help to buy his wedding suit, Alpheus approached him. Isaac's response was, "You will have to earn that money like everyone else. You can work for me and you will be paid wages to use however you wish." I guess he worked for his uncle because he was able to purchase a length of 'Chale-au-pain'[118] material, which my mother told me was tailored by his schoolmate at CTC, Lenny Langford.

In 1944, Alpheus, now the proud father of three children, returned to Cumana Village to introduce his children to their grandfather. Mother told me, "During our visit to your Grandpa, it seems he noticed that my ring finger was bare. He looked at your daddy and said, "Boy, you mean to say you're married with children and your wife has no ring?" He gave your father some money, more than enough, to buy a gold ring for me." Daddy bought the ring which he gave to my mother, and which she passed on to me in her later years.

My mother's ring today remains one of my most cherished possessions. Then there is the china basin which sat on our basin stand,[119] in a manoeuvrable space between the living and dining rooms. It went along with a tall, white, pitcher which was always filled with water. There was soap and a towel for visitors to wash their hands. The basin which belonged to Grandpa James Scobie was wrested from his home by Uncle Joe and given to my father when Grandpa died.

---

118 Appendix X (b) The recycled cotton bag in which flour was bagged for shipping. These bags were used to make bedding, clothing, underwear, and for various other domestic purposes.

119 Basin Stand made for holding a wash basin and water pitcher, eventually disappearing with the advent of modern indoor plumbing. "Sink." Wikipedia, The Free Encyclopaedia. Wikipedia, The Free Encyclopaedia, 19 Aug. 2021. Web. 15 Sep. 2021.

Home Sweet Home

Daddy was a colporteur by vocation. By 8:00 a.m., he was bathed, dressed and out of the house. His usual attire was a white short-sleeved shirt, black or midnight blue trousers, black brogues and dark grey or black socks. If the shirt was long-sleeved, he wore arm-bands to keep the cuffs from chafing against his wrists and becoming both soiled and worn. If not, I observed how my mother would 'turn the cuffs,' and darn them. He used bicycle clips to prevent the bottom of his trousers from being caught in the bicycle chain, and being covered with oil, or worse yet, torn.

Donning his cork hat, all white and cleaned with *blanco,*[120] Daddy took his brief bag, packed with books for his customers, got onto his bicycle and rode away for a morning of work. He returned home by 12:30, or no later than 1:00 p.m. if delayed, to have lunch. He did this four or five days a week. Sometimes he just took a ride on Sunday, to visit his friends Alfred Lewis and his wife Iris at Nonpareil, Oropouche, off the Eastern Main Road. After I began attending secondary school when I was around eleven years old, Daddy traded in his bicycle for a small motorbike.

My mother was a housewife who did cooking, washing, ironing and various domestic duties which she taught us girls. She also taught us embroidery, crocheting, and piano playing. Sometimes she supplemented my father's income with her crochet work and piano lessons. Most of her time, however, was devoted to keeping an immaculate home and caring for her family. We were vegetarians in accordance with the teachings of Ellen G. White. My mother had no difficulty in preparing vegetarian dishes, she was superlative at preparing food; she could spin a meal out of air, unlike my father who would burn water if given the chance. A thrifty wife who could stretch a dollar to infinity, her culinary skills were only one of her many assets.

My father, on the other hand, was the parent who saw to it that we did our chores. Our brothers did outside tasks like sweeping and keeping the yard clean. Daddy was very handy around the house which kept down maintenance expenses, but he also liked to work; he abhorred idleness. He repaired his own shoes with tools he may have learned to use while at CTC with its very expansive self-help curriculum, or he may have been self-taught. Apart from a hammer and shoe tacks, he owned a 3-way shoe last with pieces for the heel and two sole arms. For some reason we called it a 'blakey.' Later he discovered Evo-Stik glue which smelled like chewing-gum, and had a similar consistency except that the colour was pale yellow. It was recommended for bonding almost any material including leather and rubber. We were never out of Evo-Stik.

My parents were not well-off, but we lacked nothing. My father's faith was the foundation on which his life was built. It taught him to be disciplined and industrious. The strict routine practised in our household when I grew up was

---

120 A white chalk-like substance used to whiten canvas items. It was most effective when rubbed against the still wet canvas, like crepe soles. Otherwise water was added to give it a paste-like consistency.

Daddy's letter of the law interpretation of religious doctrine espoused by the Seventh-Day-Adventist denomination. It is noticeable that the zeal displayed by the converted is much less evident in the originators of the faith. All the visits and family camaraderie that took place when relatives visited did not detract from or interfere with my father's principles. He was unwavering in ensuring the strict adherence by every child in his home to daily devotions and to keeping *the Sabbath*. This was followed by a second commandment of doing well at school. Our lives were defined by a clear routine of school and church, church and school.

My father's insistence on academic excellence bore good fruit. Seven of his eight children successfully completed secondary school, graduating with the Cambridge School Certificate (HC)[121] and General Certificate of Education (GCE) certificates. The oldest child who did not attend secondary school,[122] trained as a pupil teacher, became a Certified Teacher,[123] and graduated university. One of us exceeded expectations, and went on Queen's Royal College[124] where he won a national scholarship for Modern Languages. We all became financially independent, some professionals, others with salaried occupations. No doubt my father attributed our academic success to our religious upbringing. The doctrines of the Seventh Day Adventists emphasised discipline and hard work. Our initiation into that faith began at birth and its practice continued daily while we lived at home.

All children were expected to be out of bed by 5:30 a.m. to participate in morning worship. This daily ritual started with dashing out of bed at the first notes of mother's piano playing, alerting us that there was at most three or less minutes left before the start of worship, enough time to be ready and seated. Mother's music accompanied our hymn singing, followed by a short review of the day's excerpt of scripture presented in the Sabbath School Quarterly.[125] Morning worship was not always a good time for lots of talking because we children had to get ready for school. Attendance was mandatory, except in the case of serious illness, and malingering was not tolerated. This was the day-by-day build-up to what culminated in our celebration of Sabbath at church, a mostly smooth-flowing schedule of predetermined activities.

---

121   Appendix IX (d)

122   Appendix IX (k) Exhibition examinations

123   Appendix IX (c)

124   Appendix IX (h) Queen's Royal College

125   Sabbath School Quarterly - A publication of the Review and Herald Publishing Association, a major Seventh-day Adventist publishing house in North America.

Sabbath Observance

The Sabbath per Daddy's interpretation with his vast range of biblical insight, was celebrated from sunset, usually 6:30 p.m. on Friday, to sundown at a similar time on Saturday. A full twenty-four hour period of devotion! This meant that each child was required to be at home long before sunset on Friday to *bring in the Sabbath.*

Bringing in the Sabbath was critical to Sabbath keeping. This observance started with our home, which though modest, and always attractively maintained, was given an extra dusting and polishing for the Sabbath. My role in upholding the proverb, 'cleanliness is next to godliness' manifested as I dusted the Morris chairs, plumped up the cushions, and arranged our many potted plants among them. I carefully placed my mother's white crocheted doilies on the side tables, and refreshed the pitcher on the basin stand with water and a clean towel. The wooden flooring was always polished to a high shine, (preferably when Daddy was out), by my brothers and I, wearing old socks and skidding along the parallel floorboards to peals of laughter.

After pressing my dress and polishing my shoes, I did the same for any siblings who were not at home to get theirs done on time. This was all carried out within range of mouth-watering smells wafting from the oven where one of my mother's legendary Sabbath lunches was mere minutes away from completion. Everyone showered and got dressed in clean home clothes as we children gathered in the living room to welcome the Sabbath.

This—*Bringing in the Sabbath*—was Daddy's turn to teach! He had the audience and the time, so with full authority on display, he was totally in control as he presided over the room, checking out each child under his bespectacled gaze (probably quite proud of his well-behaved brood), while passing on insights gained during his almost incessant perusal of Seventh Day Adventist literature.

It was a mini service in which all, without exception, had a speaking part. I had already placed each person's bible and songbook on their respective seats before we began by singing a Sabbath Song from the Church Hymnal[126], one of which was,

> *"The sun rolls down the distant west, Soft twilight steals abroad*
> *To welcome in the day of rest, The Sabbath of the Lord."*

Each child had a turn in weekly rotation to read a short passage from one of the revered Ellen G. White's writings, as others commented on the passage.

I did enjoy these weekly family gatherings.

The church we attended was a cosy little grey building, at the corner of Adventist Street and Ojoe Road. The Adventist Elementary School, a separate two-story building, was located at the back of the church. When

---

126 The Church Hymnal OFFICIAL HYMNAL OF THE SEVENTH-DAY ADVENTIST CHURCH Copyright,1941, General Conference of Seventh Day Adventists Hymn #59.

the congregation grew, infants, young children and juniors were housed in the school building for Sabbath School, but returned to the sanctuary before midday, for Divine Service.

My family lived within walking distance of the church, about ten minutes or so away. While walking to church on Sabbath morning, even though appearing to stare straight ahead, from the corner of my eye, I could detect the almost imperceptible shift of the neighbours' curtains which, if I turned to their direction, would seem to fall back in place as if innocently ruffled by a passing breeze. Around midday, on the way home from divine service, those who had not caught the *'early show'*, now up and about since it was afternoon, greeted my mother with an appropriately solemn, *"Afternoon Missus Scobie... and look at Bevellee!"* which we acknowledged with a slight wave of the hand, nothing too laborious on the Sabbath, mind you.

We spent most of Saturday in church where services began at 9:30 a.m. sharp. Apart from song service when everyone participated in spirited singing, Sabbath school was the most lively part of the morning. We sat in our assigned classes where everyone had a chance to participate in discussion of the Quarterly's lessons. I guess it was assumed that all class members did some form of daily devotion and reviewed those lessons during the week. Divine Service which featured the pastor's delivery of his sermon was when everyone, even those who missed Sabbath School, made an effort to be present.

Daddy even took his zeal for religious instruction to church. One Sabbath when the pastor was fumbling and mumbling, struggling to express some elusive insight, my father suddenly jumped to his feet and loudly interjected his learned opinion, using such phrases as *"erroneous doctrines"* and *"insufficient grounding"*. The congregation was visibly shocked at this startling and unexpected interruption in the middle of the pastor's sermon during divine service with a fully assembled congregation. Some who began giggling and whispering quickly settled down when the pastor resumed his sermon.

Back in those days we returned home to a leisurely lunch and rested until about 5:00 p.m. Sometimes one of us would invite one or two guests to share our lunch. The evening service, *Missionary Volunteer Service*, 'MV' which was mostly attended by younger church members, started at 5:30 p.m. and went into Vespers and closing of the Sabbath. Daddy did not attend the evening service, except there was a special feature that interested him. He and his male church cronies would reconvene at the church, around maybe 3:00 p.m. when they would expound on the scriptures, beating them to a frazzle.

Day by Day

My father kept a tight rein on us. The rigidity of his legalistic perspective on life was evident in his relationships and behaviour even with strangers outside of our home. One day while riding to work, his motor-bike was hit by a car. As he lay in the middle of the road with his motorbike nearby, good Samaritans rushed over to help. Daddy's emphatic response was, "I am not getting up! I am waiting for the police!" Despite the well meaning efforts of passersby, he was insistent as he repeated, "I am not getting up! I am waiting for the police."

The police eventually made their way to where he was, by which time a crowd and traffic had built up around the scene. The police helped him to get up and he was able to make his way back home with the help of a well-wisher. The mantra, "I am not getting up! I am waiting for the police," repeated in a stage-whisper as I walked by, became a *meme* for some less than charitable schoolmates who had either witnessed, or had heard of the accident. Even though I pretended not to hear them, the absurdity of my father's response was not lost on me. Miraculously, Daddy, apparently uninjured but shook up, and with minimal damage to his motorbike, continued to ride said motor-bike. Daddy later gave up this mode of transportation.

We were distant from our neighbours. It seemed to be an almost mutually agreed upon standoff; they weren't overly friendly either. No.1 Foster Road was the first residence in a short block of six buildings located between Cunapo and Brierley Street. Our house was flanked by Boodhansingh Rum Shop, a snackette and juke box on the left; and the Assads who owned a tailoring establishment on the right. Directly opposite us were the Sacredhan-Khans who seemed to have a large family of mostly grown sons and grand-children. They were flanked by Chow Lin On[127] grocery and dry goods store to the right; and Mrs. Wilson, a devout Catholic lady who did flowers for her Church, on the left. Her house was at the corner of Foster Road and Brierley Street.

It was taken for granted that we children generally did not socialise with neighbours, beyond a polite greeting which occasionally progressed into a full blown conversation among the adults. The Assads were chatty, the Sachredan-Khans were a bit more reserved and the Chow Lin Ons, ... Well, we patronised as needed.

When I was about nine or ten years old I realised that it wasn't just the neighbours. My school teacher invited everyone but me to her home for lunch after midday Sabbath service one Saturday. I felt that I had been deliberately left out because I was different. I knew that my father did not encourage friendships within the neighbourhood, but this was an Adventist school and

---

127 Alwyn Chow Lin On, an older son of the family, is credited with accommodating the Sangre Grande Cordettes Steelband during its nascent stages, in an unused part of the family's property where they practised at night. This was a bold move back then, when 'steel band men' weren't persons one would necessarily entertain at their home. Paul Campbell, a school teacher, was the arranger and composer for the band.

we children, I thought, were all the same. I wondered whether my parents' shared surname had set us apart as a peculiar lot. People tended to attribute characteristics to "you Scobies." I recall my father saying quite frequently, "You know they don't like Scobie." I suppose that, 'they,' were simply other people, and I detected a note of stoicism in his voice.

When I did address my *being-a-Scobie feeling* with my mother, she never denied its existence, but would say something seemingly unrelated like, "Be careful how you dress." I believe she meant that I should keep a low profile and not draw attention to myself. Much later it dawned on me that it was hardly the fact of my parents' shared surname that caused the separation because very few, if any, would have known that fact! My mother would have also known the answer to the feeling that has persisted in my adult life. I have accepted the feeling that, unless there is information to the contrary, I ascribe to my father's aura and intentionality of purpose based on his life experiences, projected onto his family, by others.

We learned how to observe the world from inside our home. We could look out onto the street and see passersby going to and fro, or funeral corteges on their way to the Foster Road Cemetery. There was very little calling out or casual conversation with someone in the street. Even so, my father sought to protect our privacy by planting ivy which grew into an impressive curtain that covered the front of the house. No one could see inside. This situation did not seem unusual, as the Chow Lin Ons, their home was completely hidden by a galvanised fence! On carnival days the bands passed in front of our house. We were certainly not allowed to participate in the carnival street processions. We weren't even allowed out of the house on those days, but we were excited onlookers who wanted to hear the music; see the costumes and catch a glimpse of a schoolmate who might be gyrating excessively. My father knew this. Our antics to see the bands passing by were probably a source of amusement to him.

The sound of the steel band would alert us that a band was coming down the road. It alerted my father too, but he was ahead of us and had already taken up his position on a chair directly in the path of the larger openings in the ivy curtain. He sat there reading his book, pretending not to notice that we were climbing over each other to see the street. I couldn't see his face, but I knew the little mischievous smirk that appeared on his face at times like this. I swear that one day I heard him singing under his breath, "If you follow Cumana boys you'll get fever".[128]

Sometimes, the constraints of our life became onerous. No one complained, but one could feel the relaxation in the air when my father left the house. On some Sunday mornings, he would go off on a mission. As soon as his back was turned my eldest sister, stepping out of her normal deportment, would open the front door and throw the top of the piano open to show off her mastery

---

128   Cheerleading song. Usually sung by the winner of a competitive cricket match. The word Cumana is
       replaced by the name of whichever village won the match.

of classical piano playing. My brother would sometimes join her in playing *Chopsticks*,[129] a delightful arrangement for solo and duet in which the players really had a chance to show off! I believe her piano playing truly delighted our neighbours. When I went by the normally poker-faced Chow Lin Ons who owned the dry-goods shop to do errands for Mother, the bravest of them took the opportunity to slyly inquire, "So who plays the piano at your home?" My mischievous response was, "All of us."

Our boredom was relieved on Saturday evenings when our parents took us younger children for a stroll through Cunapo. This stroll to me, was the equivalent to what is now a walk down Fifth Avenue in New York City. We crossed over Foster Road, to Chow Lin On Establishment - a series of wooden concertina doors, which led to what I was told were various business ventures, including the Dry Goods Shop which I knew, and a Bakery which opened onto Ojoe Road. We went by Miss Elsie, a statuesque, ebony coloured woman who sold her wares under the facade of the shop. She bore a striking resemblance to an African carving, with her colourful Martiniquan head-dress accentuating the large gold hoops dangling from her earlobes, hoops almost as large as those on her coal-pot. Her sculptured features, easing into a smile of acknowledgement, revealed matching gold teeth.

She would be busy setting-up her corner for a robust Saturday night of sales, fussing around the coal-pot, poking at the coals, while a large pot filled with yellow corns was already bubbling away on a second fire. Next to the fires there was always a tray filled with small quantities of choice, sometimes rare fruits: a variety of starch or Julie mangoes, chenette, sapodilla, sugar apple, balata, the type of seasonal fruit which made one wonder, how on earth did she get those at this time of the year? Other vendors in the vicinity paled in comparison to Miss Elsie. We crossed over Ojoe Road to Marlay, an even bigger dry goods shop; here the politely impatient watchman, carefully shepherded last minute customers outside the wrought-iron accordion barriers, the outer level protection for the inner wood panelled doors, while miraculously keeping the very late ones out. Sometimes a smaller figure wiggled by, escaping his divided attention.

Next we stopped at, The Red Store, a high-end variety store, the crowning glory of Sangre Grande and a treat to look at. The imposing storefront had large picture windows framed by red borders. This setting accentuated the clearly visible display of attractive merchandise, clothing, shoes, and dresses, along with toys, a draw for young children. The Red Store was owned by the McCarthy family who occupied a ranch style spread further up Foster Road, close by the Cemetery. After feasting our eyes on the goods where I pointed out which doll I wanted, we went by the almost invisible doors of Salim's Second-hand Store which Daddy frequented. I was my usual chatty self, eagerly spelling out the lettering on neon signs, letters I had learnt during my alphabet lessons with Mother.

129   "Chopsticks," Wikipedia contributors. "Chopsticks (waltz)." Wikipedia, The Free Encyclopaedia. 30 Nov. 2021. Web. 1 Jan. 2022.

We walked by other less impressive but also attractive showcases: Bata Shoe Store, Capil-Nath Furniture Store, all the way to the Post Office at the corner of the Eastern Main Road and Brierley Street. Although the walk was no more than about three small blocks, back then to a small child's perception, the distance seemed very far. We crossed to the opposite side of the street to make our way back, briefly stopping to look at more displays of various business establishments: Bissoondath, Cockburn's (Pioneer) Drug Store, Herrera's Drug Store, Khan's Bookstore, Lee Tings, Barclays Bank and Chow's Bakery. Here we crossed through swirling traffic at the Roundabout as my father tightly held my hand. We were back to where we started, No. 1 Foster Road, via the Roundabout.

Impressions

It is true that my father was stern, and to some he seemed unapproachable. To me, he was simply my father. The fourteen year age gap between my oldest sibling and myself appears to have created a significant difference in the range of perceptions, how older siblings viewed my father compared to how I did. The gravity of impact seemed to decline in severity, in proportion to each additional sibling coming between us. I cannot speak for my brothers and sisters, but I was close to my father.

I spent time with Daddy as he did his chores around the house. I watched him repair his shoes. In time, I was able to do a little cobbling of my own, whenever my shoes laughed, as we said when the soles become separated from the tops. I positioned my shoe on the arm of the shoe last as I observed Daddy doing and closed the gap with a bit of Evo-Stik glue first, then small shoe tacks. If they were canvas I used the glue only until new shoes were possible. We were never out of Evo-Stik.

I even picked up some of my father's speech peculiarities. Daddy had a lot of words and a lot of points to make. He was not always precise in his pronunciation of unexpected syllable combinations, some of which I repeat to this day. For example, when terrazzo tiling became popular and the more fancy sounding word patio was used instead of verandah, he mentioned 'paysho' as in the mathematical term "ratio" but with a "p". This elicited soft sniggers, and an Oh dear! smile. His articulation may have been similar to that which evolved out of the Toco region of Trinidad where I never lived, or from Tobago, whichever, like my father, I remain impervious to attempts 'to correct' my accent.

Daddy taught me to ride his motorbike, allowing me to take an occasional early morning spin all by myself along the Toco Road! While writing this work I realised that he, like his father James, owned a bicycle, a self-reliant means of transportation. He graduated to a motor-bike, a step beyond his father! Daddy also bought bicycles for the last three of us children to ride to school when we attended North-Eastern College, Sangre Grande.[130] He taught me how to patch the tires in case they were ever punctured.

When I completed elementary education and moved on to secondary school, I participated in extracurricular school activities. I would constantly gauge the time devoted to Friday activities like school sports. I represented House C (the best house!), at North Eastern College. Running the 60-yard dash and the second leg of the girls' relay was an exercise in footwork anxiety which, even when we won, persisted while I hurriedly gathered my book-bag, trotting off the field to make it home with barely enough time to get ready for—*the Sabbath*. Christmas parties were not even a voiced thought as those started after six o'clock, coinciding with the time to be at home, getting ready to celebrate—*the Sabbath*.

The sunset-to-sundown routine gradually became an irritant. As a child I was okay with the routine because I had nothing to forsake; this was all I knew. As I grew older, the parties started even later, and I felt as though I had been left behind in another space. Most of my teenage years, when not at school, were spent at the Sangre Grande Public Library feeding a voracious appetite for a variety of reading material, whatever caught my interest.

At this point I volunteered and joined the *Sunshine Band*, a group of church members who would pre-arrange to show up at a venue and sing *sunny songs* to cheer-up our audience, usually shut-ins. I was enthusiastic about missionary work. I guess I was influenced by Daddy's example! I even became one of a two-person team who gave out tracts and did Bible studies with shut-ins, patients at the hospital, and interested members of the community.

Missionary work took place on Sabbath, between 2:30 p.m. and the start of the evening service at 5:30 p.m. If I happened to be at home after 5:30, we closed *the Sabbath* by singing,

> *"Day is dying in the west; Heaven is touching earth with rest; Wait and worship while the night Sets her evening lamps alight Through all the sky..."*[131]

which, as I grew older, morphed into,

> *"The only one who could ever reach me was the son of a Preacher Man"*[132]

There was always the jukebox in the background. The music coming from this machine in the snakette next to our home, though puzzling to me, was the medium for an alternative lifestyle in my head. Here, Daddy had absolutely no control, not over the music played, when it was played, or how loud it was played. The music coming from this machine, starting with the very worst on my father's scale, Calypso music which I am sure

---

130 Appendix IX (c) Northeastern College

131 The Church Hymnal Official Hymnal Of The Seventh-Day Adventist Church Copyright,1941, General Conference of Seventh Day Adventists Hymn #51

132 Son of A Preacher Man, 1969, sung by Dusty Springfield (April 16, 1939,- March 2, 1999). A British vocalist who made her mark as a female hit maker and icon during the 1960s beat boom that resulted in the British Invasion.

at least five of us eight children knew all the songs and their words—the very funny "Dove and Pigeon,"[133] crescendoing all the way up to, "Jean and Dinah,"[134] the worst.

In my mid-teens and the only child left at home with my mellowed parents, I was able to directly point out to Daddy that morning worship on Sabbath seemed superfluous when we spent most of the day at church anyway. From then on that practice ceased, which did not mean that my father stopped being his no-nonsense, authoritative self. When I put on a pair of pants to attend my new position as a teacher at North Eastern College where I taught for a short spell after success at the A-level examinations, Daddy strongly objected to my wearing 'men's clothing.' This gave way to a social science discussion regarding what is men's clothing and why Jesus wears a "dress/robe" in all depictions.

Sunset

The years when my mother and father were the only ones left at home, I kept in close contact with them. My mother attributed Daddy's now reduced schedule to age. He moved around on foot, maybe two or three days weekly. He left home later in the day; there was no rush to get to the dwindling number of old timers who needed his books. Whenever he went out, he continued his routine of getting dressed, leaving with his brief-bag, a now much lighter and newer version of his old leather brief-bag. He was minus his trademark cork hat, and now wore dark glasses, *darkers*.

One day, my mother received a phone call from someone in Cumana. She was told that a well-dressed, elderly man who appeared to be confused was observed wandering on the main road. On approaching him, the person recognised Brother Scobie, hence the reason for the call. My mother, unaware that Daddy had travelled to Cumana, asked if he could be put on a bus to Sangre Grande where she would have someone meet and bring him home.

Now facing the reality of ageing, Mother kept a close watch on Daddy's movements thereafter. One day while looking for a book in Daddy's library which at one time boasted several shelves of religious books, Mother noticed that the shelves looked sparse. This was when she realised that even in dementia, he followed his routine. Only now he had replaced the Adventist Conference Office as the source of the books he sold with his personal library. My mother's thoughts about Daddy's "gifting phase of colporteuring": she hoped it would "do some good" to the people blessed to receive his personal books as he would have wished.

Daddy's last years of declining health were managed in the security and comfort of his home primarily by my mother and sister with the support of other family members. They were untiring in their efforts to alleviate any

133   Dove-and-pigeon-song.pdf.http://guanaguanaresingsat.blogspot.com/2016/03/dove-and-pigeon-song.html

134   Sparrow's Jean and Dinah: sparrows-jean-and-dinah.pdf NEWSDAY SUNDAY 20 OCTOBER 2019

of his discomfort. My father left us on November 27, 1986 at the age of 76 years. My mother joined him on August 17, 2017, thirty-one years later, clear headed, and just shy of 103.

DNA Mapping[135]

The final aspect of documenting my father's maternal ancestry was pinpointing the genealogical origins of his mother, Mary's parents, Joseph Arthur and Harriet Cordner, by DNA testing and analysis of the results. To do so, any male in the direct line of descent from Joseph Arthur are good candidates, as are any females in the direct line of descent from Harriet Cordner.

The DNA test results of Samuel Arthur, the son of Isaac Arthur, and grandson of Joseph Arthur, predict that he is a descendant of the Yansi people, now living in the Democratic Republic of the Congo (formerly Zaire).[136] The Yansi people are an ethnic group in the Democratic Republic of the Congo who live in the southwest of the country and number about one million. They are matriarchal, and believe that the child is formed from the blood of the mother and belongs to the mother's clan.

The results of another male relative in the direct line of descent of Joseph Arthur, the grandson of one of Isaac's brothers, predicted he had a great-grand-parent who was 100 percent Angolan and Congolese, likely born between 1760 and 1850. Both results are bolstered by documentary evidence of Joseph Arthur, born in Barbados around 1824, whose name is entered immediately below that of another Joseph Arthur, age 23, of Mozambican nationality. The Mozambican, Joseph Arthur born in 1801, is most likely the father of Joseph Arthur, the baby, born around 1824. The baby's mother was present in Barbados where he was born, I presume she was separated (forcibly—the horrors of enslavement) from his father, present in Mauritius, a British Colonial Dependency at that time.

Mary's great-granddaughter, Gloria Scobie, a female in the direct line of descent from Margaret, the family matriarch, tested. Her results predict that she is a member of the Fang people of Gabon.[137] The Fang have a patrilineal kinship social structure and their villages have been traditionally linked through lineage. They are famed for their knowledge of animals, plants and herbs in the Equatorial forests they live in. The art works of Fang people, particularly from wood, iron and steatite, are regionally famous; their wooden masks and idol carvings are on display at numerous museums of the world.

135　Ancestry.com; 23andMe.com

136　Yansi People - "Bayanzi," Wikipedia, The Free Encyclopaedia, https://en.wikipedia.org/w/index.php?title=Bayanzi&oldid=1061905196 (accessed January 9, 2022).

137　"Fang people," Wikipedia, The Free Encyclopaedia, https://en.wikipedia.org/w/index.php?title=Fang_people&oldid=1064578369 (accessed January 9, 2022).

I was overjoyed, and experienced a sense of satisfaction when I found the record of each ancestor, likely progenitors of my DNA, strands of which I carry in varying amounts, recast, blended in the descent to me, influencing who I am. My excitement was tempered by a sense of poignancy, when I read the DNA results, which point me back to the geographic locale of my ancestors origins. As I explore my Yansi and my Fang people, I feel conflicting emotions; a sense of closure on the one hand, having called the given names of souls who once lost, survived the Middle Passage, and are revitalised in me—then there is the flicker of wanting to know more about my roots.

Most importantly I have acknowledged the existence and humanity of my ancestors.

Rest in peace. *Pumzika kwa amani* (Swahili); *laa na ndokwa* (Igbo).

Above:

1953 Alpheus at Caribbean Training College.

Left:

Caribbean Training College (CTC) 1938 Colporteur Institute. Alpheus Scobie is in the last row of the photo to the left with his head against the backdrop.

Above:
Caribbean Training College (CTC) then and now.

Above:

1941 - Scobie Family Alpheus wearing 'Chale-au-pain' wedding suit. Isabella & Florence .

Left:

1945 Alpheus with wife Isabella and children - Florence, Carlyle and Carver, taken at time of first visit to Cumana to see James Scobie, Alpheus' father.

Above:
1952 Scobie Family prior to moving to Grenada: Alpheus & Isabella, L-R Irma, Carlyle, Florence, Carver, Winnifred (Buntin) and Horace. Baby in arms is Johnny (Dale).

Above:
1980s Alpheus & Isabella Scobie.

Above:
1982 Alpheus & Isabella 43Wedding Anniversary.

Above:
Mid 60s Alpheus with motorbike

Above:
Early 1970s Alpheus reading amongst his impressive personal library.

Right:
1970s Edward Scobie with his son Earl Scobie.

Above:
1960s Carver, Horace and Dale at the front gate of No. 1 Foster Road.

Above:
1960s Carver, Horace and Dale sitting on father's bicycle.

Left:
1960s Scobie Buntin, Beverly, Horace, Irma, Dale and Carver at the front of No.1 Foster Road.

152

Above:
1960s Florence Scobie, eldest daughter of Alpheus, playing the piano at Uncle Edward's home while cousin Earl Scobie, Edward's son looks on.

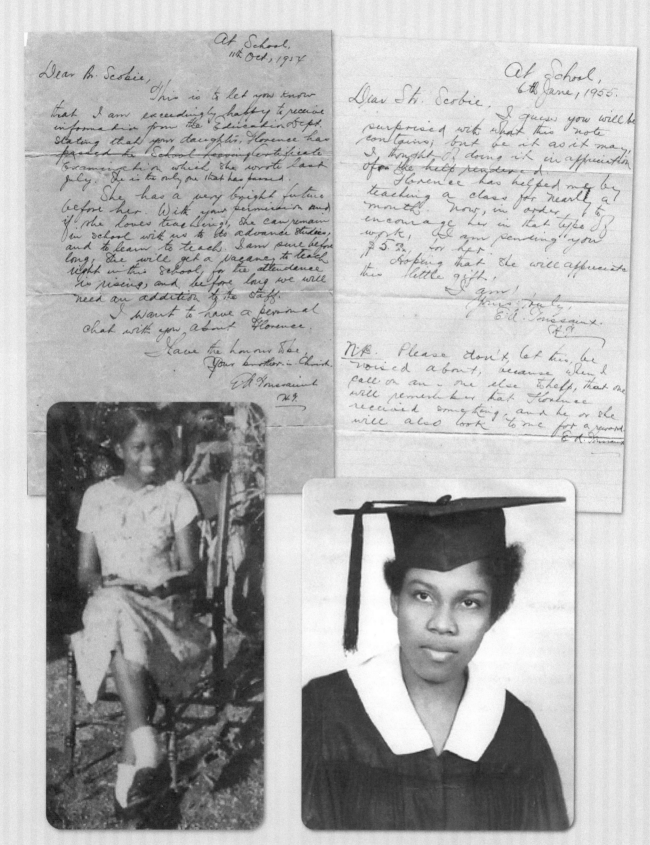

At School.
11th Oct, 1954

Dear Mr. Scobie,

This is to let you know that I am exceedingly happy to receive information from the Education Dept. stating that your daughter, Florence has passed her School Leaving Certificate examination which she wrote last July. She is the only one that has passed.

She has a very bright future before her. With your permission and if she loves teaching, she can remain in school with us to do advance studies, and to learn to teach. I am sure before long, she will get a vacancy to teach right in this school, for the attendance is rising, and before long we will need an addition to the staff.

I want to have a personal chat with you about Florence.

Have the honour Sir,
Your brother in Christ,
E.A. Toussaint
H.T.

At School,
6th June, 1955.

Dear Sir, Scobie,

I guess you will be surprised with what this note contains; but be it as it may, I thought of doing it in appreciation of the help rendered.

Florence has helped me by teaching a class for nearly a month. Now, in order to encourage her in that type of work, I am sending you $5.°° for her.

Hoping that she will appreciate this little gift,

I am,
Yours truly,
E.A. Toussaint
H.T.

N.B. Please don't let this be noised about, because when I call on any one else to help, that one will remember that Florence received something, and he or she will also look to me for a reward.
E.A. Toussaint

1953 Scobie "Flo" Florence.

Florence "Flo" Scobie graduated CUC 1963.

154

General—27A

COLEGIO ADVENTISTA
DEL PLATA
PUIGGARI
F.C.U.
(ENTRE RIOS)

Ministry of Education & Culture,
Alexandra Street, St. Clair.

No..................
In replying the above
number and date of
this letter should be
quoted.

4th August, ...19....71

To Whom It May Concern:

This is to certify that Mr. Horace Scobie
is the holder of an Additional National
Scholarship awarded by the Government of Trinidad
and Tobago and is a student at the University of
Toronto, Canada reading for a B.A. Honours degree
in Latin American Studies.

Mr. Scobie has been given permission to
spend the third year of his course in Argentina
and Brazil. While there the Government of Trinidad
and Tobago will be responsible for his upkeep and
the payment of his University Fees.

The Government of Trinidad & Tobago will
appreciate any assistance given this student.

Permanent Secretary,
Ministry of Education and Culture.

Above:
1970 Horace Scobie in his QRC uniform. Scholarship
letter from the Government of Trinidad and Tobago.

Above:
Queen's Royal College.

Carlyle Scobie graduated CUC 1966.

Above:
1970s Alpheus and Isabella Scobie.

CONCLUSION

This has been a long journey for me. I set out wanting to know more about my ancestors whose lives have influenced who I am. Specifically, I wanted to explain the puzzling issue of my parents' shared surname. I decided that I would focus on my father's maternal ancestry as a starting point.

I was able to trace my father's lineage back to Margaret Cordner who was enslaved on a plantation in Tobago, and was able to identify successive generations up to my father and his siblings. Even though I did not gain any information directly pertaining to my father's mother from 'the Arthur men,' to whom I was referred by Cousin Lee, it turns out that the stories Samuel Arthur shared with me, helped me to contextualise the significance of his father Isaac Arthur's contribution to the Toco region, in relation to his times. I did unravel the details of my parents' relatedness, but that discussion belongs in another volume which I am currently documenting.

The stories I relate here, most of which I was unaware of before I began this work, revealed gripping, fascinating and at times difficult new information for me. The experience has clarified for me a significant part of who I am, a leaf on my family's tree, my father's daughter, and a part of this history. As the researcher narrating these stories, I got the unique opportunity to introspect and observe while documenting some of who I am, and some of whom my ancestors were.

I had learned of the horrors of slavery in my high school West Indian History course. I knew that it was a system which had deleterious effects on the enslaved population. The older relatives whom I knew seemed healthy enough, but I approached the details of earlier ancestors with some apprehension. So, I was overjoyed to find Joseph Arthur, the family patriarch. It is easy to forget that he had been enslaved for all of his formative years. His thwarted attempt at insurrection showed him to be a man of exceptional character, possessed by the courage of his convictions. To me, he was so much more than a mere fire-brand. After his incarceration, he went on to become an upstanding citizen in Tobago and fathered Isaac Arthur whose legacy is still evident in Toco today.

Names like Isaac Arthur and Peter Cordner, his uncle, are written into the history of Toco among those who provided the much needed labour for a thriving agricultural village after Emancipation. Less is known of Peter Cordner who made the treacherous sea journey to Toco from an early age. It was through his efforts that his mother, his siblings and their children were able to escape the hardship of economic decline in Tobago. Isaac Arthur, on the other hand, is remembered as a proprietor and businessman whose interventions resulted in several community developments including the cemetery, post office and recreation ground. He won government contracts in the building of roads in Rampanalgas Village.

My feeling of pride in my relatives was somewhat diminished by the absence of women among the memorable Toco folk. Auntie Annie, Isaac's sister, is recalled as a proprietor who took over her brother's shop and of course Auntie *"Becca"* Rebecca who *"adopted"* my father Alpheus after his mother's incapacity. Later on, some female relatives would continue businesses started by the men. The women seemed stoic to a fault, uncomplaining as they absorbed their disappointments while supporting the family unit. This might have been the case of Margaret, the family's Eve whose heart-rending response to the fracturing of her family involved injury to her son. Nothing more is said of her, and I wonder whether she ever recovered from her loss. Church records of her daughter Anna's death suggest that hers was a reasonably respectable life. I only hope that this was so. But then there was Rebecca, Margaret's granddaughter, said to be lightheaded.

Instances of mental illness, particularly among women, is one of the more difficult revelations I came upon in these stories. I have mentioned some instances of its appearance, misdiagnosis and treatment. The complexities of addressing its origins, or distinguishing it from the effects of institutionalised infliction of trauma, a feature of the institution of slavery, I leave to the work of experts in a different forum. I continue to be appalled by the treatment meted out to those who were deemed mentally ill. I wonder if my grandmother Mary was simply in a state of postpartum depression when she tried to swim back to Tobago, and whether she might have recovered at home with simple kindness and affection. I shudder to think of her fate at the mental institution where Jacob, Isaac's son, died while undergoing surgery on his head.

Whatever the cause of the mental illnesses in these relatives, there is little doubt that they lived in difficult circumstances. The earliest of them had come into a strange land with labour as their only resource to build lives from the ground up. Survival demanded industry. Those who strove for success had to be single minded and resolute in pursuit of their goals. I think of my father and his uncle Isaac, men of different generations and world views—my father deeply religious, his uncle more worldly. Uncle Isaac had an imposing physical stature, good looks, charm, and possibly some savings he had amassed as a youth going back and forth to work on the estates. My father lived his life intentionally. He had an undiluted faith in God and practised a strict adherence to the teachings of the Seventh Day Adventists. Both men were stern, practical, legalistic and inflexible. As fathers they were strict disciplinarians who sought, each in his own way, to impose their formidable sense of purpose and order upon their children.

Every one of my father's children exceeded him in academic and professional achievements. Uncle Isaac did not have the same success in his field. He had worked hard to acquire land and businesses in Toco. His sons left Toco, leaving only a daughter and other relatives to carry on his legacy. I wondered about this. Samuel, Isaac's son, came to believe that the harsh treatment he received as a child—going to school barefoot, doing difficult chores from an early age, and such—were his father's way of moulding him into an industrious, disciplined man. Yet he, like so many other young men, chose city life and sometimes floundered.

So many questions arise and remain unanswered for there is no one to answer them. This is part of the reason that, while I am aware of the imprint of other nationalities, non-African ancestors, present from the very beginning and scattered throughout succeeding generations, I have not tried to find them. Who could possibly tell me about my great great great-grandfather Arthur Cord(i)ner, the slave owner, or his sons and their generations?

I continue to research my family's history as I document *'The Scobie Enigma'* - the paternal ancestry of my father and mother. I am piecing together what seems a jigsaw puzzle, inserting tabs where I can see the outlines of a picture emerging...

Left:

Old Police Station, Sangre Grande - Between 1900 and 1901, the Old Police Station, referred to as, "Sangre Grande Constabulary Station" was built. A small jailhouse was erected next to it. The station was demolished in 2005.

(Paria Archives, Fern Mackenzie Collection)

Above:

Warden's Office and Magistrate's Court

In the early 1900s, the building which housed the Warden's Office on Toco Road was reconstructed to a new two-story building, which now included accommodation for the Magistrate's Court. This 2013 photo shows what the building must have looked like when Samuel attended court with his father Isaac Arthur in the late 1930s. The building was demolished in 2017.

Above:
1930s Marlay & Company - Dry Goods Shop. (Paria Archives, Fern Mackenzie Collection)

Above:
2013 Marlay & Company - Dry Goods Shop.

Above:

2011 Old Fire Station, Brierley Street, Sangre Grande. In1909 the Old Fire Station was built. The building was demolished in 2017.

Above:

2013 Corner of Brierley Street and Ojoe Road.

Above:

2013 Old Post Office, Sangre Grande. In 1898 the Old Post Office was erected in Sangre Grande at the corner of River Road and the Eastern Main Road. This landmark building was demolished in 2017.

Above:
2010 Old Post Office Manzanilla - Classic "Gingerbread House". In 1909 the Old Post Office at Manzanilla was built. The building was demolished in 2017.

APPENDICES

Appendix I

(a) The Roundabout located in the middle of Cunapo, the business district of Sangre Grande, was an elevated, white circular island, the center of a Y-shaped hub, around which traffic flowed. The Roundabout today symbolizes the customary flow of traffic associated with the area. The Police Station sits between the right and left forks in the hub, overlooking the traffic flow through Cunapo. Traffic from Port-of-Spain in the West flows along the Eastern Main Road, converging with traffic from Manzanilla and beyond on the South-east, and traffic from the Toco Main Road on the North-east. Foster Road starts mere yards away to the right of the Police Station, running perpendicular to the juncture of Toco Road and the Eastern Main Road. The Roundabout is a distance of some thirty-five miles from Point Galera, Toco, the North-eastern tip of the island.

(b) Police Station: The Old Police Station, Sangre Grande, built between 1900 and 1901, was referred to as, *"Sangre Grande Constabulary Station."* A small jailhouse was erected next to it. In the 1960s, a tall pink poui tree, which appeared to be very old, stood above its facade. The tree was home to a population of corn-birds, whose nests hung among its branches, appearing like long forgotten presents on an abandoned Christmas tree. Some believe that the corn birds stopped nesting in its branches, after a famous boxer from the area thought it was a great idea to attach Christmas lights to the tree. The station was demolished in 2005.

Appendix II

(a) Arthur, Samuel Jonathan, (August 1926-April 2022) Samuel and I met in person during 2017 at the home of his son in Blanchisseuse, Trinidad. This was seven years after my initial conversation with him in 2010, while researching and documenting my father's matrilineal history. During our many conversations thereafter, Samuel recalled his father's story to me, a significant part of our family history. He was intent on having his father's story told. I hope I have effectively conveyed his sentiments, and captured the essence of Isaac Arthur's aura.

(b) Mrs. Victoria Cojer-Pritchard was a schoolmate of Samuel Arthur in the 1930s when they both attended the Cumana RC School. She is a retired educator who is familiar with some of the events described in these narratives. She fact-checked, and also provided invaluable additional information concerning the layout of Cumana Village. Recalling her time as a young lady, she stated that she frequently travelled on the *"Within The Time"* bus to Sangre Grande. When she became a Pupil Teacher Trainee, she sometimes caught the train to Port-of-Spain where she taught school. Mrs. Cojer-Pritchard currently resides at Cumana Village.

(c) **Craig-James, Susan**. *"Notes on the Sangre Grande Courthouse and the Toco Main Road."* Personal Communication to writer on June 3, 2020 regarding the Sangre Grande Courthouse and the Toco Main Road as it was being constructed.

(i) **The Sangre Grande Courthouse**

Port-of-Spain Gazette (POSG) 23 Feb. 1922, p. 11:

"Work on the Warden's Office at Sangre Grande is near completion. It is expected to be ready by the first week in March. The Warden's Office will be provided by converting the Court House to a two-storey building, the upper floor for the Warden's Office. The Magistrate's Court had been temporarily transferred to the building of the Mutual Help Society, and has resumed sittings at the regular Court House."

POSG, 9 Mar. 1922, p. 7:

"The Public Works Department (PWD) work on Sangre Grande Court House and Warden's Office is nearly complete."

(ii) **The Toco Main Road**

POSG, 9 Apr. 1922, p. 13.

"'Candid Comments' expects Toco Road to be finished by the end of May 1922. PWD is working from both Toco and Sangre Grande ends. There is now only ¾ mile of bridle road, but crossed by deep ravines, etc. Road will open up a fertile country, and help to solve Tobago's transport problem."

POSG, 20 May 1922, p. 5.

"Toco Main Road is likely to be finished in six weeks; it will be motorable by cars, trucks, buses, which would be able to ply from Port-of-Spain to Toco and back."

POSG, 17 June 1922, p. 11.

"Governor expected to open the Toco Main Road for wheel traffic; will travel from POS to Toco by car. Before the official opening, 'Quite an unusual number of strangers was seen here during the past week, Portuguese and Chinese forming a fair proportion.' "The oldest known *'Carter'* in Toco, Darling Barbast, bought a bus licensed for seven passengers for use in Toco."

Appendix III

(a) Tapia Hut - The traditional dwelling of Amerindian or First Peoples. The walls of the hut were made of earth and other organic material mixed with water, and pounded into a thick paste by villagers trampling the material with bare feet. The resulting 'tapia' was used to plaster the frame of the hut, fashioned from tree branches and bamboo cane. The process of plastering tapia, called 'lepae' (pronounced leepay), is a specialised form of moulding, which if not done correctly caused air-pockets to form within the mud walls as they dried. Jack-spaniards would nest in the air-pockets. The roof of the hut was made of the carat or timmit palm, but if either was unavailable, the coconut palm was used. The palm leaves were stripped off the branches and woven into compact sheaves which were layered and attached to a frame, forming the roof.

(b) The Clay Oven - Described by Samuel Arthur was ideally made of a mixture of white clay and sand. The oven base comprised a wooden stand on which lumps of wet clay were packed to a height of about fifteen inches. The clay was moulded into a U shape; the inside scooped out and the walls smoothed, leaving sufficient space to accommodate different sized pots. A small opening at the top of the mould to which a funnel shaped extension was added, allowed gases and smoke to escape during cooking. The wet mould was fired and left to bake. After cooling, the oven was ready for use. The clay oven was impenetrable by water and impervious to fire, which made it the ideal receptacle for cooking.

(c) Cart - A heavy two-wheeled vehicle, commonly without springs, drawn by mules, oxen, or other animals, used for the conveyance of heavy goods or passenger transport. Also a box with one or two wheels attached, which was pushed or pulled by hand.

(d) 'Suzie & Sambo' - The names given to the apparatus—a coconut grating machine and the iron pot used to make coconut oil as described by Samuel Arthur.

Isaac constructed a coconut grating machine by chiselling two sturdy blocks of wood into circular shapes, one larger than the other. He had the blacksmith bore holes into each piece, through which a length of metal was threaded, forming wheels. The metal piece formed an axle, which anchored both wheels in place, while retaining the ability to turn freely.

He covered the larger wheel with a sheet of metal perforated with small, triangular shaped holes. This perforated sheet served as a grater, and was placed over a trough box. The smaller wheel on the far end balanced the machine. Kernels were fed from a tray onto the grating wheel, to which a handle was attached to turn the wheel. This action desiccated the kernels forming meal which was collected in the trough box. Isaac built an alternative foot pedal which could be used to crank the wheel instead of the handle.

The grating wheel was covered to avoid spills of juice and meal. When the trough box was full, the meal was removed and placed in a large container, to which water was added. The mixture was then strained, the meal removed, and the remaining liquid coconut milk left to settle overnight. The curd was poured into an iron pot (Suzie) and left to boil until it changed into a clear oily substance, coconut oil.

Appendix IV

Population Statistics - "In 1891 there were 3,307 Tobagonians (1,774 males and 1,533 females) in Trinidad and 16,942 in Tobago. In 1901 the comparable figures were 5,334 (2,948 males and 2,386 females) in Trinidad and 17, 241 in Tobago. This means that between 1891 and 1901, persons born in Tobago living in Trinidad increased by 61.3 per cent; and the proportion of Tobagonians living in Trinidad rose from 16.3 to 23.6 per cent. The increase in Tobagonians in Trinidad between 1891 and 1901 was five times the increase of the Tobago population."

Craig-James, Susan, *The Changing Society of Tobago, 1838-1938 A Fractured Whole Volume II: 1900-1938* p 189.

Appendix V

(a) **Back Street** - Prior to the construction of the Toco Main Road, Back Street was the main thoroughfare in Redhead and the focal point of Cumana Village. The St. Ninian Anglican Church and the Seventh-Day-Adventist Church were located along this road. The Arthurs, Cordners and Scobies lived on Back Street, while other relatives; McClatchies, Saunders, Staffords, and Wheelers lived in the immediate environs. The street ran parallel to what would become the Toco Main Road.

Mrs Cojer-Pritchard recalled, "Walking north on Back Street, just beyond the Adventist Church, there was a river with a narrow bridge. Further on the street forked into two branches; one branch leading to the Toco Main Road, and the other leading to Morne Cabrite Trace which became known as *'Toco Old Road.'*"

The construction of the Toco Main Road brought about major changes to Redhead and Back Street. The new road proceeded on what was described as 'a more direct route' to Toco Village. Redhead was subsumed into Cumana village, and Back Street was bypassed; the bridge and river at the northern end of Back Street disappeared during repurposing of the Allendale Estate. The Toco Main Road replaced Back Street as the main thoroughfare.

Isaac Arthur's shop, which he gave to his sister Annie, was located at Cumana Village Junction. Even though abandoned, it is still standing at its original location.

Allendale Estate: It is likely that Allendale Estate was one of the big cocoa estates in the Cumana area, which spawned communities like Redhead in its environs. The estate was later repurposed and sub-divided for residential use.

Morne Cabrite Trace/Road - also known as the 'Toco Old Road, was the most direct path to get to Cumana Village from the Toco Depot and the Police Station before the Toco Main Road was built.

(b) **Soucouyant Story** - One villager who asked not to be named, recalled stories of a *soucouyant habitué* at the South Bank of the Tompire River when she attended primary school. This soucouyant was thought to be responsible for the black and blue marks which mysteriously appeared on the bodies of some villagers. On one occasion when her classmates were discussing the black and blue marks and the possible causes — a *soucouyant*, one classmate chimed in that he saw his mother muttering and going through changes before she suddenly disappeared for hours, and was back home by morning!

Appendix VI

(a) **The Family Oral Tradition** - Arthur and Cordner descendants told stories of Margaret, the family matriarch, her two sons and daughter Anna, fathered by slave owner Arthur Cord(i)ner. Two of Anna's children Peter and Harriet Arthur née Cordner, repeated these stories to their children—Wheelers, Cordners, Staffords and Arthurs. In 2009 during a Family gathering, the stories of Margaret and her children, and Peter Cordner's pioneering ventures were spoken.

(b) **Relatives who were interviewed**:

Arthur, Catherine, is the daughter of Levi Arthur, the son of Joseph Arthur Jr. Catherine shared her family stories and photos, including one of herself when she was crowned Miss St. David in 1958. (Each region hosted its own Carnival Celebrations during the 1950s, 1960s and after.) Catherine and I maintain regular telephone contact, and we visit during my trips to Trinidad.

Arthur, Greta, the daughter of Isaac Arthur shared photos of herself and her father with me during my visit to her home at Rampanalgas Village in 2010. This was the original location where Isaac Arthur lived and kept shop. The business now includes a Hotel and Conference Centre, which Greta keeps alive through extended family members.

Arthur, William *"Bill"* **Merrit**, (1938-2020) was the grandson of Colonel Arthur, Joseph Arthur's youngest son. His brother was Dowling Arthur. In 2010, I visited Bill at his Cumana Village home, when he shared family stories with me.

Arthur, Heather, daughter of Tim Leopold Arthur, mentioned her father and his brother's company, *"Arthur Brothers"* during our telephone conversation on 8/8/2010.

James, Victoria Leyonce (September 26, 1920-December 6, 2013) *'Cousin Lee,'* was the daughter of Rebecca James née Arthur, the niece of Mary Scobie née Arthur and cousin of Alpheus Scobie. During her retirement, I visited her at her Boston home, and later at Queens, New York where she relocated prior to her death in 2013.

Lewis, Roger, son of Neville Arthur, allowed me access to his DNA Results to assist in identifying familial connections. We maintain regular contact.

McClatchie, Gilbert *'Nick'* (who died on July 1, 2020), the great-grandson of Peter Cordner, grew up in Cumana Village during the 1950s and 1960s. Nick took me to meet some of our older relatives, and to see some of the places around Cumana Village mentioned in this narrative.

McClatchie, Carl *'Carlie'* (1953-January 15, 2022), the great-grandson of Peter Cordner, grew up in Cumana Village during the 1950s and 1960s. He shared his extensive knowledge of Cumana Village and surrounding areas with which he became familiar at a very young age. Carlie reported walking long distances, to and from different locations to collect produce from the gardeners who worked on his parents' land. He did 'weekly runs' with his mother, to the Port-of-Spain farmers market.

Phillip, Knolly (July 27, 1933-July 11, 2013) was the first son of Amelia Phillip née Scobie, my father's sister. During visits to Knolly and his family at their Sangre Grande home, he shared family stories with me.

Phillip, Paul 'Pablo,' *'Barbirolli,'* (10/1939-11/4/2014) was the son of Amelia Phillip née Scobie, and Knolly's younger brother. During visits to his home between 2010 and 2013, he shared family stories with me, including the one of Mary Scobie.

Saunders Murrell, Doreen (May 2, 1937-January 24, 2015) was the granddaughter of Simon Saunders, Rebecca Saunders née Cordner' son. We met in 2010 at London, England where she lived.

Scobie Tuitt, Eunice is the daughter of Joseph Scobie, my father's brother. She was one of my mother's boarders.

Scobie, *'Linroy'* **L.A. Roy** (September 19, 1948-February 25, 2014) was the grandson of Emelda Scobie, my father's oldest sister. Linroy supported the Family Tree by introducing me to family members, and curating old family photos which he shared with me. The photos he shared include those of Peter Cordner and his wife Catherine Elliott, Joseph Arthur and his wife Phillipa, and Cornell Arthur.

Stafford, Rufus aka *'Cap' 'Hero'* (April 9, 1926-December 28, 2010) was the son of Ernestine Stafford née Cordner, and the grandson of Peter Cordner. He and my father were second cousins. I interviewed him in August 2010 when he shared stories of James Scobie with me.

Stafford Quashie, Una (who died in 2015) was the daughter of Ernestine Stafford née Cordner, the granddaughter of Peter Cordner, and the sister of Rufus Stafford. During 2010 I visited her at her Cumana Village home, when she shared family photos and stories with me.

Appendix VII

Joseph Arthur - I found Joseph Arthur, described as a 1½ year old baby owned by James Corbin of Barbados in the Slave Registers of former British Colonial Dependencies 1813-1834. Baby Joseph Arthur's record is immediately below that of another Joseph Arthur, age 23, of Mozambican nationality in the island of Mauritius, a British Colonial Dependency. The older Joseph Arthur is described as a Personal Slave owned by Daniel McKay. Apart from the inference that the baby Joseph Arthur belongs to the adult of the same name, the Christian and surnames of both do not include any part of the name of their owners, McKay and Corbin. [It was not unusual for the owner to give his name to his slaves, and if baptised, the slave's name was included with the owner's surname]. The similar names lead me to question whether the baby is the child of the adult? Did Daniel McKay of Mauritius sell the pregnant baby's mother to James Corbin of Barbados? Was the baby's mother brought to Barbados while pregnant? Eight years later in 1834, the baby Joseph Arthur is now registered as a 9½ year old boy owned by James Corbin of Barbados.

Sometime post Emancipation, it appears that this was the same Joseph Arthur who migrated to Tobago, when, In January 1854, a plot to burn and pillage the town of Scarborough, was discovered by the confession of an accomplice. Two of the ringleaders, emigrant negroes from Barbados, Joseph Arthur and Thomas Millington, were arrested and each was sentenced to imprisonment for two years, and a fine of 10 pounds: and on completion of their imprisonment they were to find security for good behaviour for six years, remaining in prison until such security was given ... Millington was threatened with blindness, and he was released... On 5th April, 1858, Lieutenant-Governor J.V. Drysdale, exercising the royal prerogative released Arthur from his confinement: and the latter became thereafter a model citizen of Tobago (Archibald, Douglas. p 29-30.)

Appendix VIII

(a) Cocoa House - An A-framed structure similar in appearance to a house, built on some cocoa estates for processing cocoa beans. The cocoa house was usually built away from the main residence, partly to avoid the pungent smell of fermentation and the insects it attracted. The walls were made of wooden slats, designed to maintain a humid temperature within the house. At the widest part of the A-frame, metal strips were attached to parallel joists and wheels fastened to the joists, which allowed for movement of the roof. Grooves carved into the floor were fitted with rails to facilitate moving the roof over the rails. Raised extensions or flaps on the sides kept the roof from sliding off. An operator could safely slide the roof back and forth over the floor to allow the beans which were spread out on the floor, to be exposed to sunshine, or prevent them from being wet by rain. The cocoa house was supported on wooden stilts or large stones.

(b) Sweating Cocoa - Cocoa seeds when extracted from the pod are embedded in a white cotton like pulp which is removed to process the seeds. Sweating is triggered when the seeds are stored in the tightly sealed cocoa house where the combination of heat and moisture generates high amounts of humidity, causing them to sweat. Sweating loosens the pulp from the seed, at the same time triggering fermentation which enhances the taste of the bean. After sweating, the roof of the cocoa house is retracted, and the seeds left to dry in the sun, during which time they are intermittently raked and re-spread, allowing for maximum exposure to the sun. Any pulp that remains after drying, disappears during *dancing the cocoa*.

(c) 'Dancing Cocoa' - is a form of threshing which removes pulp from the cocoa seed, especially any pulp which had not dissolved during the drying process. Sometimes a solution made of *bois cano* plant leaves soaked in water was sprinkled on the seeds before dancing. The solution acted as a polish, intensifying the sheen on the beans, which made them more attractive and sale-able.

(d) Chocolate - Trinitario, is an exclusive variety of cocoa that was conceived in Trinidad during the 18th century. Trinitario is the world's most exclusive cocoa hybrid— and one of the rarest— representing only 5% of all cocoa. Another 5% of the world's cocoa production belongs to Criollo, the finest pure cocoa in the world. Criollo and Trinitario, the two finest and most rare cocoa varieties, only grow in 23 countries, 8 of which are in the Caribbean. 100% of cocoa exports from Grenada, St. Lucia, Trinidad and Dominica consist of either Criollo or Trinitario.

Ewing-Chow, Daphne, Senior Contributor Food & Drink, forbes.com *"The Caribbean Fine Chocolate Industry Is About To Explode"* Aug 24, 2019, 04:14pm EDT https://www.forbes.com Start Citation in new line.

Appendix IX

a) **Caribbean Training College (CTC)** - emerged in 1927 from the institution known as the Eastern Caribbean Training School (ECTS) which was founded sometime in the early1920s. In 1935 my father Alpheus Scobie attended CTC when the physical footprint of the institution like its mission was evolving. Recruits were encouraged to bring along simple building or agricultural tools, more specifically *"a cutlass or hoe."* Everyone participated in the on-going construction of the college which focused on dissemination of the Gospel and Life Skills. In 1956 Caribbean Training College transitioned to Caribbean Union College (CUC) as its curriculum expanded. Four of Alpheus's children attended the College, following in his footsteps - to further their education and training. The institution up until 1970, had a reach of almost the entire English, French, and Dutch speaking Southern Caribbean, Central and South America. In 2006, the University of The Southern Caribbean (USC) superseded all prior iterations of the institution.

(b) **Primary Level Education** - referred to as 'the three R's'—Reading, Writing and Arithmetic, basic education—was available at Borough and denominational schools. Learning from standards I through VII was available, but some students completed standards I-V, or somewhere in-between. Those who completed standards VI and VII, and passed the School Leaving Certificate Examination, along with other subjective criteria, could pursue a teaching career through Pupil Teacher Training.

(c) **Pupil Teacher Training** - A process of supervised classroom training where the trainee known as a *'Monitor,'* during the first year, was required to complete Parts I, II and III of evaluative examinations in successive years. Learning on the job and an additional two years of training at a Teacher Training College was the final step to becoming a Certified Teacher.

(d) **Secondary Level Education** - also called *'High School'* was reserved for those whose parents could afford to pay fees. A very few top performing students who excelled at the College Exhibition Examinations were allowed entrance to selective secondary schools on scholarships. All other students paid a fee to attend private, mostly denominational high schools. All students private or otherwise were required to do the nationally recognised Cambridge School Certificate examinations, referred to as the Higher Certificate (HC) which marked the successful completion of secondary schooling. When government funded secondary schools were established in the 1960s, secondary schooling was made available to all; entrance hinged on passing the Common Entrance Examinations, which replaced the College Exhibition examination.

The HC Examinations were replaced with the General Certificate of Education (GCE A-Level and O-Level) Examinations. Completion of five-years of secondary schooling, and passing grades in at least five subjects at the GCE O-Level was required to pursue an additional two years of A-Level schooling. The few secondary schools which offered the additional two years of advanced level schooling were mostly located in Port-of-Spain.

(e) **North-Eastern College** - in Sangre Grande founded in 1961, is one of the secondary schools created in the 1960s which made secondary education accessible to all. It is now a seven-year educational institution. The initial five-year curriculum was expanded to 7-years in 1967; the General Certificate of Education Advanced Level was made available and students now had the option to pursue advanced level schooling in Sangre Grande. Prior to its establishment, four siblings (second through fifth) attended Bates Memorial High School, while the last three of us children attended North-Eastern College. The first of us three to attend North-Eastern College, achieved top marks in the O-Level examinations and was admitted to QRC, where he went on to achieve a National Scholarship. See p 155.

(f) **Dasent High School** - was a private secondary school, established around 1941 by Eastlyn Errol Dasent, a private citizen. The school was located in Sangre Grande and offered secondary education to students from in and around the Counties of St. Andrew and St. David. The name of the school was later changed to St. Andrews High School.

(g) **Bates Memorial High School** - located in Sangre Grande, Trinidad, was established by the Seventh Day Adventists in 1951. It remains one of a few denominational and private High Schools which offer secondary level education in the counties of St. Andrew and St. David.

(h) **Queen's Royal College** - established in 1859 in Port-of-Spain, Trinidad, is considered one of the premier secondary schools in Trinidad and Tobago. In 1870 the school was called the Queen's Collegiate School, and was housed in the Prince's Building. Students were taught algebra, geometry, arithmetic, geography history, Latin, French, English, Greek and Spanish. This was the first school in the Caribbean and outside of England to participate in the Cambridge examinations. In 1902, the school was relocated to its present address at Hayes Street, Port-of-Spain, where the main building is considered one of the Magnificent Seven - a group of historic buildings built around the Port-of-Spain Savannah in the early 1900s. The school became known as Queen's Royal College. Admission is based on performance in the top percentile of the Common Entrance exam when students move from primary school to secondary school. QRC prepares students for the Caribbean Examination Council Certificate (CXC) at 5th Form and the Caribbean Advanced Proficiency Examinations (CAPE) on completion of the seven-year secondary education curriculum.

(i) **St. Mary's College** - established in 1863, is popularly known as CIC, for College of the Immaculate Conception. It is a government-assisted selective Catholic secondary school situated on Frederick Street in the heart of Port-of-Spain, and is considered one of the premier secondary schools in Trinidad and Tobago. Admission is based on performance in the top percentile of the Common Entrance exam when students move from primary school to secondary school. St. Mary's College prepares students for the Caribbean Examination Council Certificate (CXC) at 5th Form and the Caribbean Advanced Proficiency Examinations (CAPE) on completion of the seven-year secondary education curriculum.

(j) **Presentation College** - located in San Fernando, was started in 1930, and is considered one of the premier secondary schools in Trinidad and Tobago. Admission is based on performance in the top percentile of the Common Entrance exam for students to get from primary school to secondary school. Several students are awarded National Scholarships, which are highly selective merit-based grants. Students who qualify for these scholarships would have attained the highest grades in the Caribbean Advanced Proficiency Examinations (CAPE) taken upon the completion of a seven-year secondary education curriculum.

"Presentation College, San Fernando." Wikipedia, The Free Encyclopedia, 18 Sep. 2021. Web. 4 Jan. 2022.

(k) **Exhibition Examinations:** In 1951 at the age of 11 years, my oldest sister Florence began secondary education at the fledgling Bates Memorial High School. The School shared space with the SDA Primary School in a one-story building located at the corner of Adventist Street and Ojoe Road, Sangre Grande. In 1952 my father was 'called to Grenada,' a missionary call which he accepted. The family settled at Victoria, where my sister went on to win the island wide exhibition to attend the prestigious Grenada Girls High School in St. George's, the island's capital. My father was unable to secure boarding accommodation for her with an Adventist family, and thought it best to return to Trinidad where he hoped his daughter's academic excellence would be recognized and gain her a scholarship to Bates Memorial High School. On the family's return, my father did not get the reception he expected and he was unable to pay the required school fees. My sister had no other choice for schooling except to resume attendance at the Primary School she had previously left. She became the only student at her school to pass the School Leaving Examination in 1954 (See letter dated 1954 from School Principal - E. A. Toussaint).[133] My sister entered the Pupil Teacher System and graduated as a teacher. Unknown to her at the time, Knolly Phillip,[134] our cousin who attended the Sangre Grande Roman Catholic Primary School, won an Exhibition to attend St.

---

133 See Letter dated 1954 at p 154.

134 See Appendix VI (b) p 171, Relatives interviewed - Knolly Phillip.

Mary's College, Port-of-Spain. His success did not work out well for him either. It seems that even though he was a Roman Catholic and attended a Roman Catholic School, he was denied admission to St. Mary's College because his mother was not a Roman Catholic! Both cousins unaware of each other's achievements and disappointments at the time, became aware during conversations many years later.

Appendix X

(a) **Cabell *"Cab"* Calloway III**, (December 25, 1907-November 18, 1994,) was an American jazz singer, dancer and bandleader, who famously performed at Harlem's Cotton Club in New York. He called the *zoot* suit, *"the ultimate in clothes."* With its super-sized shoulder pads, sprawling lapels and peg leg pants, the *zoot* suit grew out of the *"drape"* suits popular in Harlem dance halls in the mid-1930s. The flowing trousers were tapered at the ankles...by the '40s, the suits were worn by minority men in working-class neighbourhoods throughout the country.

"A Brief History of the Zoot Suit; Unravelling the jazzy life of a snazzy style". Alice Gregory; April 2016. https://www.smithsonianmag.com/arts-culture/brief-history-zoot-suit/ accessed January 1, 2022.

(b) **"Chale-au-pain"** (pronounced '*shallowpeah*'), is one of the names for the recycled cotton bag primarily used to bag flour for shipping. The recycled bags were used to make bedding, clothing, underwear, and for various other domestic purposes. Though not generally admitted (flour bags were considered, *"poor people's clothes"*), its use was quite common during the 1930s and beyond. Chale-au-pain may have been a word used to prop up and or disguise the common flour bag. The Great Depression of 1929 and beyond, along with the overlapping World War II which began in 1939 and ended in 1945, had devastating effects which trickled down to the British Colony of Trinidad and Tobago. Goods previously available from Europe and North America such as fabric for clothing, were now scarce or unavailable. Innovative citizens resorted to recycling cotton bags to substitute for the fabric used to make clothing. The practice of recycling flour bags for domestic use was also common in the United States of America - *"1930s Flour Sacks Featured Colourful Patterns To Make Dresses"* | LittleThings.com.

BIBLIOGRAPHY

23andMe https://23andme.com.

1813-1834 All Slave Registers of former British Colonial Dependencies The National Archives of the UK; Kew, Surrey, England; Collection: Office of Registry of Colonial Slaves and Slave Compensation Commission: Records.

1813-1834 Slave Registers of former British Colonial Dependencies, [database on-line]. Provo, UT, USA: Ancestry.com Operations Inc, 2007. Slave Registers of former British Colonial Dependencies 1813-1834. Ancestry.com.

1856 Will of Robinson Scobie, father of James Scobie. (copy).

1863-1946 Baptisms Parish of St. Andrew & St. George 3/1863-4/1873Baptisms St. George Parish of St. George 4/16/1873-11/3/1946Baptisms Tobago 1897-1914 Whim, Adelphi, Parlatuvier.

1865-1886 Register of Burials in the Parish of St. Andrew & St. George, Tobago. Burials 1888 St. Andrew 1884-1899 St. James & St. Peter 1899-1944 St. George Chapel 1873-1914

2010 St. Andrews Anglican Church, Churchyard Cemetery, Scarborough Tobago.

2010 National Archives, Kew Gardens; Collindale Reading Room, London, England The Tobago Chronicle and Royal Gazette Vol. VI Scarborough, Tuesday October 24, 1839. Records of the Colonial Office - Original Correspondence; Newspapers and Early Official Gazettes: reports of runaways, slave auctions, sales of property (including slaves).

2010 & 2011 National Archives-105 St. Vincent Street, Port-of-Spain, Trinidad. 1781-1817 English Protestant Church of Tobago. Register of Baptisms, Marriages and Burials

Ancestry https://ancestry.com. DNA tests for Ethnicity & Genealogy DNA Test.

Anthony, M. (1988). Towns and Villages of Trinidad and Tobago. Circle Press.

Archibald, D. (2003). Tobago *"Melancholy Isle"* Volume III 1807-1898. WEST INDIANA. p 29-30.

Besson, G. A. (2013, August 19). The Cedula of Population. The Caribbean History Archives. https://caribbeanhistoryarchives.blogspot.com/

Besson, G. A. (2008). Folklore & Legends of Trinidad and Tobago (4th ed.). Paria Publishing Company Limited.

Besson, G. A. (2011, November 3). The Mayaro Soucouyant. The Caribbean History Archives. https://caribbeanhistoryarchives.blogspot.com/ Besson, G. A., & Brereton, B. (2010). *The book of Trinidad. Trinidad and Tobago: Paria Publishers*

Brereton, B. (1996). An Introduction to the History of Trinidad and Tobago. Heinemann Educational Publishers.

Campbell, Carl. C. (1966, The Young Colonials: "The Dual System of Education in Trinidad From 1875 - 1890" A Social History of Education in Trinidad and Tobago, 1834-1939 Press University of the West Indies.

Craig-James, Susan E., The Changing Society of Tobago, 1838-1938 A Fractured Whole Volume II: 1900-1938

Ewing-Chow, Daphne, Senior Contributor Food & Drink, forbes. com *"The Caribbean Fine Chocolate Industry Is About To Explode"* https://www.forbes.com

Gregory, Alice (April 2016) "A Brief History of the Zoot Suit; Unravelling the jazzy life of a snazzy style". https://www.smithsonianmag.com/arts-culture/brief-history-zoot-suit/

HouseOfNames.com - Cordner Spelling Variations

LittleThings. com. ...The practice of recycling flour bags for domestic use was also common in the United States of America - "1930s Flour Sacks Featured Colourful Patterns To Make Dresses"

Meredith, Mark, *"Toco's Turning Tide Part III"* Sunday Express, 19 May 2019, p 4.

Morton-Gittens, Dane History in Action, Vol. 2 No. 2, September 2011ISSN: 2221-7886 The University of the West Indies (St. Augustine, Trinidad and Tobago) Dept. of History The Golden Age and Decline of Matelot, Trinidad (1885-1945)

Ottley, C. R. *Complete History of the Island of Tobago in the West Indies. Guardian* Commercial Printery, Port-of-Spain, Trinidad, B.W.I. retrieved from The Schomburg Center for Research in Black Culture. New York, New York.

Review and Herald Publishing Association https://www.reviewandherald.com

The Turtle Trust. Sea turtle conservation. turtlevillagetrust.org

Wheeler Family, Oral Tradition, (2009) Family Reunion Document.

Wikipedia, The Free Encyclopaedia.

Williams, E. (1963). Documents of West Indian History: From the Spanish discovery to the British conquest of Jamaica. PNM Publishing Co., LTD.

Williams, E. (1970). From Columbus To Castro: The History of the Caribbean 1492-1969 (First Vintage Books Edition). Vintage Books.

"To be ignorant of what occurred before you were born is to remain always a child. For what is the worth of human life, unless it is woven into the life of our ancestors by the records of history?"

Marcus Cicero